SCOTTISH HIGHER H

GERMANY
1815–1939

Jim McGonigle

Hodder Gibson

A MEMBER OF THE HODDER HEADLINE GROUP

The Publishers would like to thank the following for permission to reproduce copyright material:

Photo credits
akg-images 2, 10, 11, 12, 14, 16, 26, 28, 33, 36, 37, 38, 40, 51, 53, 57, 59, 61, 64, 67, 71, 75, 79, 82, 84, 88, 97 (both), 101, 102, 106, 111, 113, 118, 120, 122, 127, 129, 130, 133; akg-images / Erich Lessing 5; Lauros/Giraudon/Bridgeman Art Library 21; Archives Charmet/Bridgeman Art Library 24.

Artworks by Jeff Edwards.

Every effort has been made to trace all copyright holders, but if any have been inadvertently overlooked the Publishers will be pleased to make the necessary arrangements at the first opportunity.

Although every effort has been made to ensure that website addresses are correct at time of going to press, Hodder Gibson cannot be held responsible for the content of any website mentioned in this book. It is sometimes possible to find a relocated web page by typing in the address of the home page for a website in the URL window of your browser.

Orders: please contact Bookpoint Ltd, 130 Milton Park, Abingdon, Oxon OX14 4SB. Telephone: (44) 01235 827720. Fax: (44) 01235 400454. Lines are open from 9.00–6.00, Monday to Saturday, with a 24-hour message answering service. Visit our website at www.hoddereducation.co.uk. Hodder Gibson can be contacted direct on: Tel: 0141 848 1609; Fax: 0141 889 6315; email: hoddergibson@hodder.co.uk

Cover photo
Typeset in 11/14pt Sabon by Pantek Arts, Maidstone, Kent
Printed and bound in Italy

A catalogue record for this title is available from the British Library

ISBN 10: 0 340 90699 5
ISBN 13: 978 0 340 90699 6

Contents

Contents

in the NABs, the exam and even the extended essay. It is therefore well worth finding out how to write a good essay.

Any essay you write must have a beginning, a middle and an end.

The beginning is your introduction. This is where your essay takes life – or starts to struggle; it's where you must do the hardest thinking, if not, your essay will probably decline into storytelling – gaining at best a C.

Your introduction must:

- make clear that you understand what the question is asking you to do.
- make a brief reference to the title and state the decision or opinion you intend to support
- signpost the main ideas or arguments you will develop or explain in the middle section of the essay.

TIP: *Revise for assessments by planning and writing brief introductions (about seven lines) to essay questions. Word-process them so that you can return to them later to alter or refine them. The exact wording of the question you prepare might not come up in an exam, but since the topic is likely the ideas will remain useable.*

The middle part of an essay is the longest. Aim for:

- several paragraphs, and leave an empty line between each paragraph. Good clear layout makes an essay easier to read and less difficult to mark.
- a new paragraph for each new point or idea.
- a key sentence to start each new paragraph which outlines what the paragraph will be about.
- paragraphs which show off your knowledge about the subject. The detailed knowledge contained in the paragraph must be relevant to the key sentence.
- a short, one-sentence summary at the end of each paragraph which links to the main question and makes clear to a marker the link between what you have written and the main title.

TIP: *As you are writing ask yourself, 'Why am I writing this information?' If you can't make a clear link between your information and the title of the essay, it's unlikely a marker will be able to.*

Your conclusion:

- must sum up your ideas
- must answer the question
- must be relevant to the question
- must support the ideas you put in your introduction
- should prioritise your main ideas so that you make clear what you think the most important points were.

TIP: *It is perfectly acceptable, and often preferable, to reach a balanced point of view rather than completely support one point of view.*

Introduction

Who this book is for

It is for anyone taking Higher History and in particular the Later Modern period, which is the option studied by the vast majority of students.

Why was this book written?

It was written to provide an easy-to-read textbook for students who are aiming not just to pass their exam but to pass well. Other books are either difficult to read and contain far too much content, only provide basic information in pass notes style or are not written specifically for the Scottish Higher History course. This is the first full and accessible text book series for this part of the Higher History course.

What is in this book?

It covers all you need to know about the section on Germany in the Later Modern option of your Higher History course. All of the syllabus is covered so you can be sure all your needs will be met.

Why are there various activities at the end each chapter?

Research in learning proves that if you just read as a means of learning, after 24 hours you will only have retained about 10% of the new information. Unless learning is reinforced it does not become anchored in either your short-term or long-term memory.

If, after reading, you attempt an activity which requires you to use the information you have read and process it in a different way than it was presented in this book, then your memory will retain over 60% of your reading. That is why each chapter has an activity, the intention of which is to provide effective learning techniques to help acquire and reinforce knowledge. These activities can be applied to any topic with some slight adjustments. Some of the earlier activities in particular try to establish good essay writing skills.

Each chapter also ends with typical exam essay questions which will give you an idea of some of the ways the topic can be approached.

How to write a good essay

In the Higher History course, the unit on the growth of nationalism 1815–1939 is always assessed by asking you to write an essay. That is true

1 The German States in 1815

Introduction

Following the defeat of the French Emperor, Napoleon I, on the battlefield of Waterloo, the representatives of the victorious powers of Britain, Prussia, Russia and Austria met in Vienna to decide the fate of Europe. They had no clear plan of what they wanted to achieve, but they knew what they totally opposed – the forces of nationalism and liberalism which had upset the traditional balance of Europe for almost a quarter of a century. However, the settlement reached at Vienna about the shape of Europe after 1815 was a great disappointment to many. This was particularly the case in Germany where the idea of nationalism had helped inspire the people to rebel against the French.

What was meant by nationalism? In simple terms, nationalism was the idea that people with a common culture, language and history should have the right to rule themselves. Putting this idea into practice was much more difficult to achieve, and nowhere was this more noticeable than in the German states.

Germany after the Napoleonic Wars

There were many problems in achieving this nationalist aim. The first, and perhaps the most crucial, was the exact definition of Germany. In the past, the Holy Roman Empire had occupied much of central Europe, and many of the German states had been part of it. In fact there were almost 400 semi-independent states within the empire. But the old Holy Roman Empire had been in decline for many years and its organisation was chaotic. Napoleon swept the old empire away and reorganised the states into 39 larger states. He then formed the most important of these states into the Confederation of the Rhine. This, on the surface at least, resembled a more modern German state. However, the allies who met at Vienna were determined to rid Europe of as much of Napoleon's legacy as possible, and thus the Confederation of the Rhine was unacceptable to them.

The solution was the formation of the German Confederation, also known as the *Bund*. In effect, this was a loose association of Napoleon's reorganised 39 states. The *Diet* (parliament) of the *Bund* met for the first

Source 1.1

Convention of Vienna by Jean-Baptiste Isabey

time in 1816 but it had no real control over the individuals living in each of the separate 39 states and the main concern of its members was protecting the interests of their individual states, not working together for the common good. Thus, the actions of the *Bund* were to prove a bitter disappointment to German nationalists.

How did the formation of the *Bund* help to keep Germany divided?

> *The Bund was more a means to perpetuate (keep alive) the division of Germany.*
>
> Ian Mitchell, Bismarck, 1980.

What does Mitchell mean by this? Extracts from the Act of Confederation that set up the *Bund* show how difficult it would be for Germany to become united within such a structure.

> *The sovereign princes and the free towns of Germany, including their Majesties, the Emperor of Austria and the Kings of Prussia and Denmark, unite in a perpetual union which shall be called the German Confederation.*
>
> — *Article 1 of the Act of Confederation.*

By including non-German groups, the potential for self-interest and disagreements was increased.

> *The aim of this confederation shall be the maintenance of the external and internal security of Germany as well as the independence of the individual German states.*
>
> — *Article 2 of the Act of Confederation.*

There was also, therefore, a contradiction between the interests of the individual states and those of the whole Confederation.

What was the German Confederation?

The Confederation was made up of representatives of the 39 German states, who were nominated by their respective rulers. All decisions had to be unanimous.

> *The affairs of the Confederation shall be managed by a Federal Assembly in which all members of the Confederation shall be represented by their ambassadors, who shall each have one vote.*
>
> — *Article 4 of the Act of Confederation.*

This posed a considerable challenge within such a diverse group of politicians as agreement was difficult and total, unanimous agreement was virtually impossible.

The chairmanship of the *Bund* was given permanently to Austria. This was partly as a reward for being on the winning side in 1815, partly due to being considered the major German power and mainly because it was fiercely against the new ideas of nationalism and liberalism.

The Austrian emperor had set himself the task of creating a powerful Austrian Empire centred around the Danube River. Under the permanent chairmanship of Austria, the *Bund* did little to further the cause of German unity. Austria feared that nationalism and liberalism would destroy its multi-ethnic empire and so it could be guaranteed to act against new ideas and change and to work as a repressive force throughout the *Bund*. The

Source 1.2

Map showing German Confederation after 1815

Austrian chancellor, Prince Metternich, made it his policy to oppose what he regarded as the twin evils of liberalism and nationalism wherever they should appear. He was able to maintain this position as the smaller German states were in awe of the power and position of the Austrian Empire. With absolute control over the management and administration of the empire and with the army leaders recruited from the aristocracy, Austria was able to stamp its authority and attitudes upon the *Bund*. At the same time, Metternich did not want to see the creation of a strong northern rival in the shape of Prussia and thus he sought to keep the *Bund* weak.

The threat of Prussia to Austrian domination

Prussia was the second most important of the German states. This kingdom had emerged from the Napoleonic Wars with its reputation enhanced. Prussian armies were vital in the final defeat of Napoleon and a series of military, education and economic reforms had turned Prussia into a growing, powerful state.

However, in some ways Prussia in 1815 still seemed an old-fashioned state. It was ruled by the House of Hohenzollern, whose monarchs were as unrivalled in their authority as those of either Austria or Russia, and most of its wealth at this time was based on agriculture, not industrial growth.

However in 1815 at the Congress of Vienna Prussia gained the Rhineland as well as Westphalia and Pomerania. These territorial acquisitions resulted in the doubling of the Prussian population to more than 10 million, and brought an increase in skilled labour and accessibility to raw materials for industry.

As Austrian military power and its bureaucracy continued to decline in effectiveness, its Prussian neighbour developed the apparatus necessary to build a modern state.

>
>
> *Although it was not recognised at the time, the seeds were sown for a shift in the balance of power between the two German Powers in the Vienna Settlement of 1815, which distributed territory at the end of the Napoleonic Wars. Whereas Austria acquired new possessions outside Germany (mainly in Italy), Prussia gained extensively in western Germany, and lost Polish lands to Russia, and in the process turned itself from being a state with interests mainly in eastern Germany to being the dominant power in the whole of the northern half of Germany.*
>
> *Andrina Stiles, The Unification of Germany, 1989.*

Despite the dominance of the agricultural sector within the Prussian economy, there were clear signs of the beginning of industrialisation. This was boosted when Prussia was given control of the area around the west bank of the River Rhine by the Congress of Vienna, which was rich in coal and iron deposits. At first the mainly Catholic inhabitants were not happy about being absorbed by Protestant Prussia but their opposition was gradually reduced by increasing economic prosperity. Thus began the drift in power away from Austria and towards Prussia as the latter began to build upon the rich resources available to it.

However, in 1815, Prussia was in no position to challenge the power of Austria within the *Bund*.

Source 1.3

Francis I, Emperor of Austria, from a painting by Friedrich von Amerling (1803–1887)

Obstacles to the unification of Germany

The other German states were of minor importance and tended to follow the lead taken by Austria. An additional problem which divided the smaller states was the issue of religion. The northern German states were mostly Protestant in religion, while the southern German states were mostly Catholic. The two major German states were Prussia, which was a Protestant state, and Austria, a Catholic state. Thus, small northern states were inclined to look to Prussia for help and protection, while the small southern states looked to Austria.

Nationalists were also divided over the question of what territory should be included in any united Germany. There were two schools of thought:

- The *Grossdeutschland* (Big Germany) group believed that any united Germany should include Austria, although there was no agreement on whether any part of its multi-ethnic empire should be included. Needless to say, Austria would never agree to join a united Germany without its empire intact.
- The *Kleindeutschland* (Smaller Germany) supporters believed that a united Germany should not include any part of Austria and its empire.

Thus, defining exactly what was meant by 'Germany' was a real barrier to unification.

Another obstacle to German unity came in the form of the leaders of the 39 German states. They were protective of their individual power and position and did not wish to see either lost to a rival. Therefore they wanted to maintain the status quo of their power and prestige.

A significant factor outside Germany also contributed to the difficulties. None of the Great Powers of Europe wished to see the creation of a strong Germany which might upset the balance of power. Britain, Russia and Austria were all content to see the German states weak and divided.

Such were the forces ranged against the prospect of a powerful, united Germany. Those who wished to see this come to pass had many difficulties to overcome. But they also had arguments on their side.

1

Which factors favoured the unification of Germany?

The main unifying force was language. Although dialects were common, there were about 25 million people who spoke the same language and who shared the same culture and literature. One group which supported the idea of a united Germany was the writers and thinkers of the eighteenth century. Men such as Heinrich Heine and Johann Fichte had encouraged the growth of a German consciousness.

> "
> *The separation of the Germans from the other European nations is based on Nature. Through a common language and through common national characteristics which unite the Germans, they are separate from the others… Those who speak the same language are joined to each other by a multitude of invisible bonds by nature herself, long before any human art begins; they understand each other and have the power to make themselves understood more and more clearly; they belong to one another and are by nature one and inseparably whole.*
>
> Johann Fichte, *Reden an die deutsche Nation*
> *(Address to the German nation), 1806.*

Fichte also believed that Germany had to unite for economic reasons. The industrialisation of Britain, and later France, had left the German states at a disadvantage. German businessmen wanted an end to trade barriers between the German states in the *Bund*, and also the ability to exploit all of the natural resources scattered amongst the various states. This desire was reinforced by economists like Friedrich List, who believed that the state should impose tariffs to help the development of native industries and create a national railway system for the German-speaking area. He was firmly of the opinion that economic development was helping to create a united Germany but that political unification would in turn help to accelerate the process of economic growth. Such views won widespread support amongst the intellectual middle classes, many of whom realised unification would also assist their business interests.

> "
> *The liberal creed derived its economic support from manufacturers, bankers, entrepreneurs… but its intellectual defenders generally came from the ranks of the learned professions.*
>
> TS Hamerow.

The German States in 1815

The problems that beset the early German nationalists were formidable, and at the start of the period in 1815 they were initially to prove too powerful. Despite this, nationalism and nationalist ideas continued to develop and spread throughout the German states.

Activity

1 Using the information given, write a summary of the forces that opposed nationalism in the German states at this time, explaining the reasons for opposition.

2 Now complete the same task for the forces in favour of a united Germany.

3 At this stage, what is your assessment of the likelihood of a united Germany being formed relatively quickly?

The Rise of Nationalism

Introduction

When the representatives of the victorious powers from the Napoleonic Wars signed the Treaty Of Vienna in 1815, they might have been forgiven for thinking that their task was complete. The traditional rulers of the European states had been restored, and as far as possible the boundaries had been redrawn to turn the clock back to 1789 before the wars with France began. The twin forces of liberalism and nationalism seemed to have been defeated.

Some things had changed. The old Holy Roman Empire had been replaced by the German Confederation and, under the leadership of Austria, it was unlikely to support any nationalist revolt, and indeed was more likely to support conservatism and oppose further change.

> Even in 1815 there were tens of thousands of people, especially among the young, the educated, and the middle and upper classes, who felt passionately that Germans deserved to have a fatherland in the same way as the English and French already had.
>
> Andrina Stiles, *The Unification of Germany*, 1989.

Part of the reason for this was the means by which the rulers of the old European states had inspired their people to rise up to defeat the French enemy. The people of central Europe had been encouraged by their leaders to take part in a nationalist rebellion against the French invaders. But these nationalist hopes were ignored by the peacemakers at Vienna. The failure of this meeting to encourage any nationalist hopes was an important reason for support of nationalist causes after 1815.

The growth of nationalist societies in Germany

Following 1815, nationalist feelings were first expressed in the universities and amongst Germany's great writers and poets. During the wars, the universities had witnessed the emergence of nationalist student societies called *Burschenschaften*. These were dedicated to seeing the French driven from German soil and had grown since 'Germany's' success in the Battle of the Nations (or Battle of Leipzig) in 1813. Their nationalist enthusiasm tended to be of the romantic kind, passionate yet with no clear idea as to how their aims might be achieved. It could be argued that these supporters of the nationalist cause were merely following in the footsteps of earlier eighteenth-century writers. Wilhelm von Humboldt had already inspired the nationalist cause with his demands for the restriction of power of the monarch. Poets like Goethe and Heine also celebrated the idea of the nation-state. The folk tales of the Brothers Grimm celebrated Germany's past and looked forward to the day when it would at last be united in an independent nation. Their studies indicated that the German language had come from a common source. United by language, it was felt that the Germans should also be united politically. It is hardly surprising then that the authorities kept a close eye on developments within the universities, and their suspicions were soon justified.

Source 2.1

Goethe in the Roman Campagna

In 1819, a member of an extreme nationalist student society murdered a secret agent of the Tsar by the name of Kotzebu. This gave Chancellor Metternich of Austria an excuse to move against all nationalist groups and especially student societies. At a meeting of the Confederation at Carlsbad in 1819, it was agreed to set up inspectors to oversee the universities, student organisations were outlawed and a strict press censorship was enforced. These were soon known as the Carlsbad Decrees and they authorised the setting up of a commission to investigate revolutionary movements. The effect of the decrees was the dismissal of a number of professors.

> *The Carlsbad Decrees certainly succeeded in keeping Germany quiet for a considerable period of time.*
>
> Finlay McKichan, Germany, 1815–1939:
> The Rise of Nationalism, 1992.

These decrees were reinforced in 1832 when the Six Acts were passed, increasing censorship and empowering the states to take more action against any opposition groups.

Source 2.2

Student demonstration at Hambacherfest, in the 1830s

But did these ideas amongst the most educated group of people actually have much effect upon the ordinary German people? German historians have often called this period *Vormärz* (pre-March) since they regard these restrictions as part of the background causes of the Year of Revolutions in 1848. Much of the debate in these societies was theoretical in nature and probably above the understanding of ordinary Germans. Evidence does exist to show that workers, now increasingly huddled together in large urban areas, were beginning to take a real interest in politics and philosophy, but only in relatively small numbers. Thus, as Andrina Stiles comments, 'Liberalism and nationalism remained largely middle-class before 1848.'

Having managed to stifle student opposition through the Carlsbad Decrees, Metternich decided to extend these reactionary forces. When representatives

The Rise of Nationalism

of Austria, Prussia and Russia met at Troppau in 1820, they agreed to act together (the term used at the time was to act 'in concert') to suppress any nationalist or liberal uprisings that would threaten the absolute power of the monarchs. This was a bitter blow to nationalists within the German states and led to Britain distancing itself from its former wartime allies. By 1820, the forces of reaction seemed to have won.

There was another wave of student activity in the wake of the 1830 revolution in Paris. At the Hambach festival the red, gold and black colours were first used to symbolise German liberalism. These activities and demonstrations did little to advance the cause of German unification. However, beneath the surface, nationalist sentiment was never far away, as was shown in 1840.

Source 2.3

Early German satirical cartoon attack on censorship

France was trying to win the approval of the other European powers to allow it to take over Egypt. As part of the negotiations, France threatened that it would extend its eastern frontier with the Confederation to the natural boundary of the Rhine. Germany itself seemed to be threatened. Rapidly, forces hostile to the French were mobilised. What was significant was that these forces were not confined to the parts of the Rhineland that would be absorbed, nor were they limited to Prussia whose land this now was, nor were they restricted to the middle classes. For the first time since liberation from Napoleon, ordinary Germans were roused to the defence of the fatherland. The events of 1840 showed that nationalist feelings had spread to large numbers of ordinary German citizens. For its stout defence of the Rhine, Prussia emerged with great credit amongst German nationalists.

Industrial and population changes

It was actually in the area of economics that the German states first experienced the benefits of some form of unity.

The early 19th century was a time of great change within all European states. Indeed, it has been suggested that the political changes of the nineteenth century can only be explained by an understanding of the social and economic developments of the time.

What did Thomson have in mind?

> No social and political order could have remained unaffected by so immense an increase in humanity. And the events of the nineteenth century remain unintelligible unless the greatest revolution of all is kept constantly in mind.
>
> David Thomson, Europe since Napoleon, 1965.

Firstly, the population of Europe grew rapidly during this period. As in Britain, this increase in numbers led to industrialisation and the drift of country folk to the towns, looking for new employment opportunities and, hopefully, better working and living conditions. The twin forces of urbanisation and industrialisation were important factors leading to change. In the German states, the population rose from about 25 million in 1816 to over 34 million by 1845. In 1815 the number of factories was small, but by 1845 there had been a marked increase in this form of production. However, it is necessary to keep these developments in perspective as the chart below shows by contrasting German and British industrialisation.

Source 2.4

	Coal production (million tonnes)		Pig iron production (thousand tonnes)	
Period	German States	UK	German States	Britain
1820s	1.6	22.3	90	669
1830s	3.0	28.1	146	1142
1840s	6.1	48.6	184	1786

According to the census of the 1840s, only about 600,000 out of a population of 34 million were classed as factory workers. Nonetheless, it

Source 2.5

Growth of industry in Germany prior to 1848

has been argued that the forces unleashed by industrialisation did help push Germany towards unification.

Ian Mitchell suggests that political fragmentation of the German states was the most important obstacle to German economic development. He points to the existence of many different currencies, customs regulations, taxes and legal systems as examples of the difficulties that German businessmen faced at this time. These held back any attempt at modernisation.

There can be little doubt that such circumstances did hinder the growth and development of industry. Thus, it is not surprising to find middle-class businessmen of the time calling for a more united market to enable them to compete with countries such as Britain.

The effect of Prussian economic expansion

With Prussia's acquisition of land on the River Rhine after 1815, its territory was now spread across northern Germany. Prussia's control over the Rhineland, many miles away from Prussia's main territory, meant that it had good reason to try to reach an agreement with its neighbours to ensure relatively free travel of goods and people between its lands in the

east and the west. Businessmen in the Prussian-controlled Rhineland complained to the Prussian authorities about the tax burden that they had to bear when moving goods across the German states to reach Prussia in the east. This, they claimed, was holding back further developments. Ironically, they were able to take advantage of the good road network that had been set up during the period of French occupation, and wished to see this extended.

Under such pressure, the Prussian authorities agreed, in 1818, to the abolition of all internal taxes and customs duties within Prussia itself, thereby creating a large free-trade area. Taxes and tariffs were put on goods entering Prussia and the benefits of this system were that money was raised for the Prussian government to improve communications and helped meet the needs of businessmen.

> "
> *Little by little, under the direction of Prussia and because of common interests, the states which make up this union will compose a more or less compact body, acting in common.*
>
> — *Chancellor Metternich of Austria.*

Prussia also had other advantages which encouraged the other German states to reach agreements with it. For example, Prussia controlled the great rivers of the Rhine and the Elbe, which were vital communication and trade routes. Prussia's neighbours therefore needed agreements to transport of their goods along these routes. At first only some of Prussia's smaller neighbours joined, but in 1834 the *Zollverein* (Customs' Union) came into being. By 1836, twenty five of the thirty nine German states had signed up to this new economic free-trade area. Significantly, Austria was excluded from these developments. The Austrian chancellor, Metternich, saw the potential of such a customs union and objected strongly to it.

> "
> *Certainly Prussia was not thinking in terms of political unification when it founded the Customs Union. Nor had the states joined it out of love for Prussia but simply and solely to escape from the financial and economic difficulties that beset them. However, as Metternich shrewdly commented, 'Austria is on the point of seeing herself to a certain extent excluded from the rest of Germany and treated as a foreign country.'*
>
> *It would be inappropriate to see the Zollverein as the forerunner of German political unity. There is ample evidence to show that Prussia did not have it all its own way in this Union and many of the members refused to be bullied by Prussia into taking its lead or advice.*
>
> — *William Carr, A History of Germany, 1969.*

The Rise of Nationalism

There is little doubt that Prussia established the *Zollverein* purely for economic reasons. The fact that Austria was excluded from this important aspect of public finance was a political bonus.

> *The smaller states in the north now became economically dependent on Prussia's goodwill.*
>
> Ian Mitchell, Bismarck, 1980.

The effect of continued German economic and industrial growth

Further developments in the 1830s and 1840s pushed the German states into closer co-operation. The development of the railways from the mid-1830s had a dramatic impact upon the German states, ending their isolation from one another and enabling the transport and exploitation of Germany's natural resources. By 1850, over 3000 miles of railway had been laid and, as elsewhere in Europe, railways had spin-off benefits for the rest of the economy. Their development created employment opportunities in their construction phase and, later on, men were needed to run the services. Demand for coal, iron and steel all increased and the lowering of transport costs provided a boost to a host of other industries, including the cotton and woollen industries. The example of this economic co-operation between the German states did provide encouragement for those seeking a political solution to the issue of German unity.

Source 2.6

Railways in Germany prior to 1848

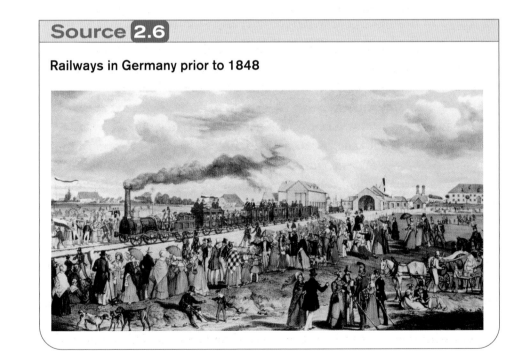

> Many modern historians support the view that from the 1830s onwards Prussia was using the Zollverein to achieve a 'Prussian solution' to the German question. Those who found financial advantage in an economic union under Prussian leadership might be expected to take a favourable view of similar arrangements in a political union. The Zollverein was a force for unity in the 1840s and therefore a focal point for nationalist sentiments. As a result Prussia, despite its reactionary political sympathies, came to be regarded by many as the natural leader of a united Germany.
>
> Andrina Stiles, The Unification of Germany, 1989.

Prussia as a leader

Prussia, ruled by the Hohenzollern family, and dominated by its Junker (Prussian nobles) farmers, had a reputation of being ultra-conservative (cautious about change), rather than a reactionary (totally against change) power. Prussia had emerged from the Napoleonic Wars with a modern bureaucracy in place and a military reputation second to none on mainland Europe. So it is perhaps surprising that nationalists and liberals looked to Berlin, the capital of Prussia, for some signs of leadership in the question of German unity.

Despite years of discussion in the 1820s and 1830s, the idea of a united Germany remained just a dream. Austria's domination of the German Confederation meant that no progress could be made on this issue and the *Bund* remained nothing more than a talking shop. But some changes were happening. In the states of south-west Germany support for liberals increased and in the state of Baden half of the elected members of the Lower House of Parliament were converted to liberal ideas. This was matched by demands in the state of Hesse-Darmstadt for changes in the rules governing elections. In contrast Prussia, under its king, Frederick William III, continued to be ruled as an autocratic state where power was in the hands of the king and no-one else. But that changed in 1840 when the King died. The new monarch, Frederick William IV, was unstable and swung between political extremes, sometimes acting as an autocrat, at other times putting forward support for liberal ideals. Initially, the liberals were cheered by the policies of the new monarch. Political prisoners were released, censorship of the press was relaxed and liberal leaders were appointed to posts within the Council of State. Encouraged by such liberal tendencies, demands for more progress grew. These included pressure for a constitution for Prussia and a single parliament to help run the country. Inevitably, such demands were too much for the new king. Press censorship was restored in 1843 and the *Junker* land owners now appeared more content with their monarch. But by 1847 King Frederick William needed

money to build a new railway linking East Prussia with Berlin. Having tried to obtain loans from various European banks, Frederick William found that without the approval of a popular assembly of representatives of the Prussian state no loan would be forthcoming. The king found himself with no option but to call a United Diet of the Prussian Estates. Given his upbringing, it is hardly surprising to find that the king expected that the assembly would give its unhesitating approval. Their demands for a constitution for Prussia and the ending of the king's autocratic, absolute rule in return for a guarantee for the loan took the king by surprise. He rejected their demands out of hand, which did little for his popularity. The scene was set for a clash between monarch and public that was to culminate in the revolutionary upheavals of 1848.

Activity

To what extent did the Zollverein stimulate nationalism in the German states before 1848?

- Decide what the question is asking you to do. N.B. the essay is not just about the Prussian customs union.

- The essay is about **all** the developments (e.g. cultural nationalism on the one hand and the role of Austria on the other) between 1815 and 1848 that encouraged German nationalism. It is necessary to show how each contributed and assess its importance.

- Try to show the marker that you know about historical debate by using a quotation in support of or against the point mentioned in the title, e.g. William Carr referred to the Zollverein as "the mighty lever of German unification".

- The answer, therefore, can be divided into two sections – factors helping the development of nationalism and factors hindering it.

- The conclusion should draw together the main themes. Try to reach a balanced conclusion that considers all the factors leading to the growth of nationalism. Mention the differences in progress between them. Finally, make clear what side of the argument you support. Was German national feeling due to economic developments?

Alternative essay options:

Assess the difficulties that German nationalists faced in achieving their aims in the period 1815–1848.

Teach a lesson

In groups of three or four your target is to teach a lesson which focuses on the 1848 revolutions to the rest of the class. Your main resource for information is this textbook but you must research widely using other resources to design an inspiring lesson. Use your experience as a student to help identify the features of a successful approach.

Negotiate with your teacher/tutor how long you have to prepare this lesson.

Your lesson should be presented in an organised, interesting, mature and informative way.

Planning is vital – and all members of the group should participate.
The lesson should last between 5 and 10 minutes.
Include any visual material, such as PowerPoint or OHP.

As in any lesson there are really important things for you to decide and aim for:

- What do you want your fellow students to be able to do and know at the end of the lesson?

- How will you assess the success of your lesson – in other words what will you expect to see or hear your students doing to prove your lesson has been successful?

Exam essays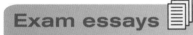

Your course work will be assessed in an exam which, in the case of Germany, will consist of one essay from a choice of four. This example provides some suggestions and advice on how to tackle an essay.

This is the title:

To what extent do you accept the view about German nationalism that 1850–62 was a time when nothing happened?

First of all decide what the question is about, but be careful! Although the question mentions Bismarck, this essay is NOT about him. It's about developments in German Nationalism between 1815–1848. What you really have to do is describe what happened to encourage Nationalism between 1815 and 1848 and then explain how important these developments were.

Your introduction must outline what you will do:

You have been given one opinion ("a time when nothing happened") and that might refer to political Nationalism after the Karlsbad Decrees.

You also know that things such as cultural Nationalism, the industrial revolution, the Zollverein and the spread of roads and railways all happened before 1848 so some things were happening. Mention all these points briefly in your introduction. You will explain all these points more fully later. All you are doing is showing the marker you know what the question means and what direction your essay will take.

Your middle section:

This is the place to demonstrate what you know.

Is there anything to support Bismarck's point of view? Point out that with the banning of the student unions after the Karlsbad Decrees, the opportunity for political Nationalism to grow was greatly restricted. You could argue that politically Austria still dominated the Diet of the German Confederation and therefore the German states, but you could then say that other types of Nationalism were growing. That is a link to your next paragraph.

Explain the importance of cultural Nationalism, giving some ways in which it was expressed. Explain how it helped spread pride in Germany and how it helped moves towards unity.

Move on to economic Nationalism. Explain how the industrial revolution changed Germany, how the Zollverein created changes that increased Prussia's power and helped make Germany more united.

It is often a good idea to show a marker that you know about historical debate by using a quotation giving the opposite point of view from the one in the title so choose something that disagrees with Bismarck. What about using a quote from historian Carr who described the Zollverein as "the mighty lever of German unification"?

In your conclusion you should:

- try to reach a balance that considers all the pressures leading to nationalist growth – economic, political and cultural.
- mention the difference in progress between them in your conclusion.
- finally, make clear what side of the argument you support. Was nothing happening after all?

Another essay option:

Do you agree that economic growth was the most important development in the growth of German nationalism before 1848?

3 1848: The Year of Revolutions

Introduction

A combination of complex economic, social, political and ideological factors led to what has since been referred to as the 'Year of Revolutions'. This chapter will seek to explain each of the factors and how, in combination, they affected the major states of the German Confederation. There can be little doubt that the events of the years 1848–1849 were to have a profound effect upon the future course of German history.

Sources of discontent

The traditional view of the causes of the revolutionary activity is that the uprising in Paris against the rule of King Louis-Philippe had a ripple effect across the whole of continental Europe. However, this version fails to take into account the various changes which were taking place in Europe and against which the traditional rulers were powerless to act. These changes

Source 3.1

WH Heine, on the barricades of Rue Soufflot

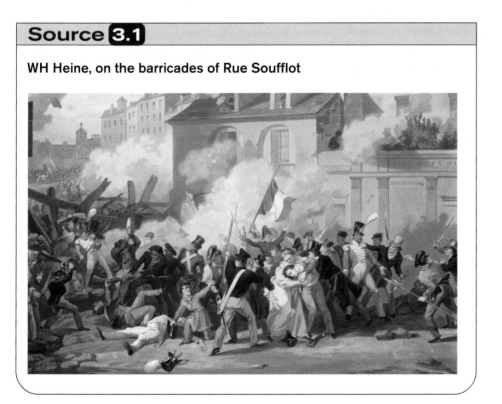

included the progress of industrialisation, with all of its negative aspects – poor working conditions, exploitation of male, female and child labour – as well as the threat posed to independent craftsmen working from home. An account of conditions in Silesia in 1844 illustrates these points:

> *Here in the villages... cotton weaving is done at home. The distress of the workers was and is not less important here... The distress and the urge to obtain work was used by individual manufacturers to the greatest possible extent in order to obtain a great quantity of goods [from the weavers] for little pay.*
>
> *A crowd of weavers appeared [at a village] and on its march attracted weavers from their dwellings... They demanded higher pay, which was refused them. It was not long before the crowd stormed into the house and smashed everything... It was solely the strength of the military power, and the infantry and artillery, and later even the cavalry, that prevented the weavers from trying any further resistance.*
>
> Wilhelm Wolf, Das Elend und der Aufruhr in Schlesien, 1844.

As a result of the decline in available work in villages more people were seeking homes and employment in the new urban centres as the following chart shows.

Source 3.2

Growth of German cities

	1800	1850	1880
Munich	30,000	110,000	230,000
Cologne (Köln)	50,000	97,000	145,000
Essen	4,000	9,000	57,000
Chemnitz	14,000	32,000	95,000
Dusseldorf	10,000	27,000	95,000

Faced with poor living conditions and high rents, working classes in the towns and cities were now much more willing to protest and demonstrate. Even in the countryside, those who remained found it difficult to make a living. Landowners had been increasing rents to such an extent that many peasant farmers were on the brink of losing their livelihood.

Additionally, there was a marked decline in the amount of food available due to poor harvests in 1846 and 1847 and, as in Ireland in 1845–46, there was an outbreak of the potato blight. Potatoes were the main diet of much of the German peasantry and the outbreak of the blight had a devastating impact. Such shortages of food had happened in the past but what made the effect even greater in 1848 was the growth of the population.

People living in the towns were faced with a shortage of food and an increase in prices at a time when many of them were losing their jobs due to the recession and thus could not afford to pay the prices demanded. This combination of higher prices, lower wages for those in employment and widespread unemployment all combined to produce a fall in the workers' standard of living.

In both the towns and in the countryside the people were unhappy at the state of affairs and began to make demands. These included a call for better housing and pay and improved working and living conditions. There were, however, no demands for political change. There was no call for democracy, liberalism or nationalism. The workers and peasants simply wanted to be able to survive from day to day and they would support any government that would improve their conditions.

It was not just the lower classes who were discontented. There were rumblings of unrest amongst the middle classes as well, for a variety of reasons. There was increasing frustration about the lack of job opportunities amongst men qualified to fill the traditional middle-class jobs of medicine,

Source 3.3

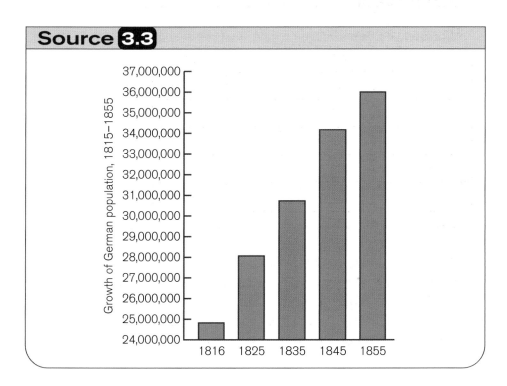

the law and civil service administrators. In most cases the senior posts were held by the younger sons of the nobility. The middle classes were also annoyed at their lack of power and influence. The ruling classes still dominated the government and they took little heed of the new ideas of liberalism and nationalism. The middle-class' demands included fairer taxation, education for all and the creation of a united German Republic.

Thus, 1848 saw a combination of differing demands from the working classes, the peasants and the middle classes but all of which had one thing in common – change.

The forces of change

Pressure for change finally came to a head in the *Bund* in February 1848 when a revolution in Paris overthrew the French monarchy. Change now seemed a real possibility and demonstrations were held in many of the German states. Such was the anger at the rule of Metternich in Austria that the chancellor of 33 years was forced to flee the city for his life like a common criminal. Austria was also faced with simultaneous uprisings of ethnic minorities within the empire, notably the Hungarians and the Italians. Within Prussia, there had been demonstrations in Berlin during which the army had opened fire, sparking off several days of street fighting. It was now that the contradictory nature of Frederick William IV became obvious. While opposed to the demands of the demonstrators, he

Source 3.4

This painting by Gemälde von F. Sorriieu (1848) shows that the forces of nationalism were present across all of Europe

was shocked by the death of so many protesters. He now appeared to accept their demands and even appeared wrapped in the colours of black, red and gold, the emblem of a united Germany.

> *To my people and to the German nation – Germany is in a state of internal ferment and can be threatened by external danger from more than one side. It can be saved from this double danger only by the most intimate unity of the German princes and peoples under one leadership. Today I take over this leadership for the days of danger… I have today taken the old German colours… Prussia henceforth merges into Germany.*
>
> — Frederick William IV, King of Prussia, 1848.

To the nationalist and liberal revolutionaries the time seemed right. With Austria distracted by events within its empire, and Prussia appearing willing to take the lead, the creation of a united Germany might just be achieved. Frederick William had even given an undertaking to co-operate with a new liberal, freer assembly whose creation was already being discussed.

Within some German states, most notably Baden, there had been moves for the creation of a united Germany. Late in 1847, representatives from all of the south-west German states had met to consider this proposal. In the revolutionary atmosphere that spring a meeting was called for March 1848 in the city of Heidelberg. The fifty one representatives from six German states, including Prussia, unanimously agreed to tackle the problem.

> *…to prepare proposals concerning the election of and the establishment of an appropriate national representation and speedily to take care of the invitations to an assembly of German men. With the prudent, faithful and manly co-operation of all Germans, the Fatherland may hope to achieve and to maintain freedom, unity and order in the most difficult situations, …*
>
> — Frederick William IV, King of Prussia, 1848.

The Frankfurt Parliament

Invitations were sent to all states to be represented at the Vorparlament (preliminary parliament) to meet at the end of March. The response to the invitation was spectacular. Five hundred and seventy four delegates met in Frankfurt and, after long debate, they agreed on the mechanism for the election of a national Constituent Assembly. This parliament would be tasked with drawing up the rules of government – or constitution – for a united Germany.

Membership of this Constituent Assembly would be based on one member for every 50,000 inhabitants and they were to be elected by appropriate

Source 3.5

The Frankfurt Assembly

means in each of the separate states. Mostly the vote was restricted to owners of property. There was no consideration given to female suffrage, and those who were poor or receiving relief from the state were to be excluded. Meanwhile the old rulers of the German states agreed to the idea of an elected parliament, but they had little real sympathy for the idea of an all-German parliament. Afraid of losing their thrones, they waited and watched until they could safely re-establish their traditional control.

The Constituent Assembly, also known as the Frankfurt Parliament, met in May 1848 but the hopes that were pinned on this body were soon dashed. From the start, the assembly was dominated by the middle-class and the well-educated – over 80 per cent of the delegates had university qualifications. Their interest lay more in a united Germany than social reforms.

The assembly also lacked teeth and relied too much on the support of King Frederick William of Prussia. At first that seemed not to be a problem when the king agreed to the new assembly's demands to push the Danes out of two states on the Danish–German border of Schleswig and Holstein. Then Frederick William changed his mind and signed an armistice with Denmark, having decided that he no longer wanted to help unite Germany through revolutionary activity. The Frankfurt Parliament had to accept Prussia's decision. The lack of an independent armed force directly under the control of the Frankfurt Parliament was a grave hindrance to the assembly who had to rely on the Prussian army to crush disturbances now occurring throughout Germany.

In the meantime, the work of the assembly proceeded at a snail's pace. All agreed that a constitution was necessary but few could agree on the exact format of that document. Given the lack of organised political parties and a lack of leadership, the assembly turned into a talking shop. But eventually a constitution was agreed. Parliament would consist of two parts, or houses. The lower house was to be elected by secret ballot and all men over 25 could vote.

The upper house would contain representatives of the rulers of the German states. Its powers would range over finance and defence and the head of state would be a constitutional emperor whose only real power would be his ability to delay any proposed legislation.

Parliament also devised the Fifty Articles of the Fundamental Rights of the German citizen. These included freedom of speech and of worship, equality before the law and an end to discrimination based on class. These were giant steps towards a more liberal, democratic and fair German society but it had taken nine months of debate to produce them. By the time the constitution was agreed, the moment had passed and the days of the Frankfurt Parliament were limited.

It is easy to sympathise with the view of the English historian, AJP Taylor when he described the events at Frankfurt as suffering, 'from too much experience rather than too little; too much calculation, too much foresight, too many elaborate combinations, too much statesmanship.'

Another problem that the assembly had to face was the exact definition of what Germany was. There were two points of view:

- Supporters of *Grossdeutschland* (Greater Germany) believed that Germany should include Austria and some even thought that part of its empire should also be included. Austria was less than enthusiastic about a united Germany anyway and the prospect of losing part of its empire did little to win its support. *Grossdeutschland* was also favoured by the southern German states who believed that a Germany including Austria would be a counter-balance to a Germany dominated by Prussia.
- *Kleindeutschland* (Lesser Germany) supporters wanted a united Germany without Austria or its empire. This solution was favoured by Prussia as the plan would make it the dominant force in any new country.

Eventually a vote was called and it was decided that Austria should be excluded. But this was by no means a clear-cut decision as the chart on page 28 shows.

1848: The Year of Revolutions

Source 3.6

Vote to exclude Austria by the Frankfurt Parliament, 1849					
By region	Yes	No	Abstention	Absent	Total
Prussia	150	30	0	17	197
Northern Germany	72	37	0	14	123
Southern Germany	39	69	0	19	127
Habsburg Empire	0	88	3	20	111
Total	261	224	3	70	558
By religion	Yes	No	Abstention	Absent	Total
Protestant	167	69	0	25	261
Catholic	42	120	3	36	201
Other	6	7	0	1	14
Not known	46	28	0	8	82
Total	261	224	3	70	558

Failure within the assembly and events external to it were to prove the downfall of the 1848 revolutions. By March 1849 the new Austrian emperor, Franz Josef, was firmly in control of his country once more. He was totally against the idea of Austria being absorbed into a united Germany and he sought to re-establish Austrian leadership within the *Bund* and restore Austria's previous total control.

Too late, the Frankfurt delegates had at last decided to offer the crown of a united Germany to Frederick William of Prussia. He too had now firmly crushed the rebels within Prussia and had no desire to fan the flames of revolution any further. Speaking privately, the Prussian king had nothing but contempt for the crown he was offered.

Source 3.7

Frederick William IV

> "
> *Every German nobleman is a hundred times too good to accept such a crown moulded out of the dirt and dregs of revolution, disloyalty and treason.*
>
> Frederick William IV, King of Prussia, 1849.

In public, he softened his words but the end result was the same.

> "
> *If accepted, it demands from me incalculable sacrifices and burdens me with heavy duties. The German National Assembly has counted on me in all things, which were calculated to establish the unity, power and glory of Germany. I honour its confidence… But I should not justify that confidence if I were to take a decision which would be of decisive importance to them without the voluntary assent (agreement) of the crowned princes of our Fatherland.*
>
> Frederick William IV, King of Prussia, 1849.

In other words, he would only have accepted such a crown if it had been offered by his fellow rulers! With Frederick William's rejection of the crown of a united Germany, the days of revolutionary activity were over. Delegates from Austria and other states were withdrawn and the assembly finally disintegrated.

Without clear aims, decisive leadership and an armed force to enforce its decisions, the Frankfurt Parliament had been unable to fulfil its revolutionary aims. To many, it seemed that a great opportunity to create a liberal, united Germany had been missed.

Why did the 1848 Revolutions fail?

First of all, the revolutionary leaders had no clear aims about what was to be achieved. There was no agreement on *klein* versus *gross-Deutschland* or whether Germany should be a monarchy or a republic.

Secondly, the German rulers maintained their authority and used it to regain their power when the tide of revolution turned. They had bought time by granting reforms which allowed them to retain control and wait for better days. More importantly they retained control of their armies. These could be used to crush any remaining revolutionaries.

Thirdly, the reforms that were granted, such as agreeing to a constitution, could be easily reversed at a later date.

Fourthly, the 'revolutionaries' were divided. Some were not even revolutionaries! Workers had been roused to action by hunger and poverty and demanded higher wages and shorter working hours. But these demands were at odds with those of the middle classes, many of whom were the employers of the workers.

Fifthly, the Frankfurt Parliament was dependent on Prussia for armed support. It had no armed force to ensure its decisions were followed.

Finally, the rulers of the 39 German states could see little for themselves in a united Germany. After all, there could only be one emperor. Self-interest led to their opposition to the actions at Frankfurt.

The attitude of King Frederick William

Despite his failure to support action in 1848–49, Frederick William was still keen on the idea of a united Germany – but only one of his creation. He wanted to increase Prussia's role and influence within the German states. He proposed the creation of a federation of the German states within which Prussia would control the army and foreign policy. In effect, they would have created a *kleindeutsch* state. These proposals were put to delegates who had assembled at Erfurt. In the meantime, Frederick William had again lost his nerve and the proposed union was still-born. Not surprisingly, Austria reacted furiously to the proposals. With control firmly re-established over its empire, Austria put forward a counter-proposal for the recreation of the German Confederation, discussed by representatives at a meeting in Frankfurt in May 1850.

Faced with Austrian opposition, and fearing that the Prussian army was no match for that of Austria, the Prussians backed down. This was confirmed at a meeting of the two rivals at Olmütz in November 1850. Thus it was agreed that the *Bund* should be re-constituted as it had been prior to the events of 1848, i.e. dominated by Austria. This agreement signalled the complete triumph of Austria and the humiliation of Prussia. It appeared that the events of 1848 had already been forgotten and that the ideals of German nationalism were now a spent force.

Activity ▶

Teach a lesson.

In groups of three or four your target is to teach a lesson to the rest of your class which is linked to the revolutions of 1848. Your main resource for information is this textbook but you must also research, find, beg or borrow other resources to make your lesson come alive. Think of the times you have been bored just listening to someone talk. Your lesson must be different!

Negotiate with your teacher / tutor how long you have to prepare this lesson.

Your lesson should be presented in an organised, interesting, mature and informative way.

Planning is vital – and all in your group must participate. It would be helpful to assign tasks such as a gopher to go get, a timekeeper to watch how your time is being used, a facilitator to keep things running smoothly in your group (tact and diplomacy needed here!) and a recorder to note ideas and what was suggested before you all forget.

Your lesson should last between 5 and 10 minutes.

It must have visual material – power point or OHP are possibilities.

As in any lesson there are really important things for you to decide and aim for:

- what do you want your fellow students to be able to do and know at the end of your lesson?

- how will you assess the success of your lesson – in other words what will you expect to see or hear your students doing to prove your lesson has been successful?

Exam essays

1 Why did the revolutions of 1848 in the German states fail?

2 How important were the revolutions of 1848 to the growth of German nationalism?

The Time When Nothing Happened?

Introduction

After the drama and excitement of 1848–1850, it is easy to understand why historians have written that this was 'the time when nothing happened'. It was a period of relative stability between the year of revolutions and the events of the 1860s leading to unification. However, it would be wrong to conclude that nothing happened between 1850 and 1862.

> The Revolution in Germany had positive as well as negative aspects... True, the men of 1848 did not attempt to build up a mass following. Nevertheless, wider circles of the population began to take an interest in politics.
>
> ... without the groundswell of public opinion favourable to unification which the revolution had created, the achievements of Bismarck in the 1860s would hardly have been possible.
>
> ... the Revolution also helped clarify political attitudes and encouraged the formation of political associations, the forerunners of modern political parties.
>
> William Carr, A History of Germany, 1969.

Changes in Austria

The decade of the 1850s saw proposals and counter-proposals concerning the future structure of German political life. These came to nothing as either they were opposed by Prussia or Austria or, on occasion, by both powers. At other times, the smaller states rejected the proposals as they feared that too much power would be given either to Austria or to Prussia.

Within Austria, events were under way to undermine its position within not just the *Bund* but internationally as well. In 1852, the dominating political force of the Austrian Empire, Chancellor Schwarzenberg, died. Austria became entangled in events in south-east Europe which meant it had to reach an agreement with Prussia. A treaty was drafted between the two powers on maintaining the traditional balance of power within the Confederation.

Internationally, Austria had made a serious blunder. By failing to support its old ally Russia in the Crimea against Britain and France, Austria lost an important friend. The Tsar, Alexander II, never forgave Austria for this betrayal. In 1849, with Austria's empire in revolt, it had been the arrival of the Russian army which had secured the day for Austria. During the Crimean War the Tsar expected that Austria would repay the favour. Failure to do so led to the disruption of Austro-Russian friendship which would never be re-established, despite the best endeavours of Bismarck in the 1880s. Russia would thus remain neutral in any future war concerning Austria, a neutrality that would inevitably favour Austria's opponents.

Source 4.1

Alexander II of Russia

Otto von Bismarck, Prussian representative to the *Bund*, was well aware of the implications of this change in the power relations.

> *He [Bismarck] wanted to use the upheaval in European power relations caused by the crisis… to enhance the power of Prussia in Germany at the expense of Austria.*
>
> Edgar Feuchtwanger, *Bismarck*, 2002.

Commenting on the disruption of Austro–Russian relations, Feuchtwanger argues that Austria had lost all hope of support from Russia.

> *The Holy Alliance (between Austria and Russia) was shattered for good and Austria had exchanged Russian support for hostility… Austria would astonish the world by its ingratitude towards Russia.*
>
> Edgar Feuchtwanger, *Bismarck*, 2002.

Domestically, within the *Bund*, there was little that Austria could do to prevent the setting up of the *Nationalverein* (National Organisation) to struggle for the creation of a united Germany. The programme of the *Nationalverein* can be seen in the declaration from August 1859.

Although such calls had little chance of success, it did indicate that national feeling was an emerging force within the German states despite

Austria's views, and within Prussia it led to the setting up of the Progressive or Liberal Party.

> *The need to subordinate the demands of political parties to the great common task of German unification have brought together from the various German states a number of men, some of them belonging to the democratic party, some to the constitutional party, for the purpose of coming to an understanding about the establishment of a constitution for a united Germany and about the necessary common course of action for the attainment of that aim. They have agreed the following points.*
>
> *The German Federal Diet should be replaced by a firm, strong, permanent central government and that a German national assembly should be summoned.*
>
> *In the present circumstances effective steps for the attainment of this aim can originate only with Prussia.*
>
> *It is the duty of every German to support the Prussian government according to his strength...*
>
> *We expect all patriots in the German Fatherland,... to place national independence and unity above party demands...*
>
> Declaration of the Nationalverein, 1859.

Changes in Prussia

The situation in Prussia was also changing slowly. Under the direction of Manteuffel (1850–1858), moderate reforms were carried out, although this did not lead to any increase in the influence which the Prussian *Diet* had on internal affairs. He centred his support on the peasant class whom he believed to be the main support of conservatism within Prussia and loyal to the monarchy. By reducing the burden of taxation and offering loans to peasants Manteuffel hoped to increase the loyalty of the peasants towards the rulers of Prussia.

In the towns and cities, the government supported schemes to help factory workers. Again, the aim was to grant some of the workers' demands, thereby encouraging them to support the rulers of Prussia and turn away from revolutionary ideas. Despite what appeared to be positive, liberal reforms Manteuffel's aim was to prevent political change. He was no supporter of liberal demands. A strict press censorship was enforced and there were restrictions on the ability of political parties to hold meetings.

> *The Manteuffel regime was a bureaucratic regime, in general committed to the maintenance of the status quo, but tempered [balanced] by the perception that the maintenance of Junker privileges in all circumstances could not always ensure stability and social peace.*
>
> Edgar Feuchtwanger, Bismarck, 2002.

Source 4.2

Coal and lignite production (million tonnes)

Date	German Confederation	Austria	Britain
1850–54	9.2	1.2	50.2
1855–59	14.7	2.2	67.8
1860–64	20.8	3.6	86.3
1865–69	31.0	5.3	104.7

Pig iron production (thousand tonnes)

Date	German Confederation	Austria	Britain
1850–54	245	173	2,716
1855–59	422	226	3,583
1860–64	613	216	4,219
1865–69	1,012	227	4,984

Length of railway line open (kilometres)

Date	German Confederation	Austria	Britain
1850	5,856	1,579	9,797
1855	7,826	2,145	11,744
1860	11,084	4,543	14,603
1865	13,900	5,858	18,439
1870	18,876	9,589	21,558

Thus, in the 1850s, Prussia presented a paradox (a contradictory impression), alternating ultra-conservatism with carrying out progressive social reforms and encouraging the economic growth of the state.

In diplomatic and political terms, the tide was moving in favour of Prussia and economically, Prussia was beginning to outstrip Austria. This would have far-reaching political, economic and military consequences for both powers.

The decade of the 1850s witnessed a growth and development of both the Prussian and German economies at the same time as that of Austria was stagnating. These developments were due, in part, to the continued development of the *Zollverein* and the discovery of raw materials in the Rhine and the Saarland, all of which were to be exploited by Prussia. On the other hand, Austria had few raw materials and was falling behind in an age where industrial strength was becoming increasingly important in politics.

Why are these figures so important?

The chart above shows the widening gap between the output of the German Confederation and Austria. Figures for Britain have been added to allow for an international comparison.

It is probably true to say that in the 1850s, few would have thought that Prussia would have unified Germany. Yet the figures clearly show that Prussia was moving ahead industrially at a rapid pace. The financial encouragement offered by the Manteuffel government resulted in a rise in

Source 4.3

The benefits of Custom Union

Das Lichten eines Hochwaldes.

industrial production and foreign trade as well as a rise in the standard of living. Although, politically, Prussia was no match for Austria, economically, the reverse was true.

In addition, it is significant that the smaller German states were in need of trade with Prussia. Working through the *Zollverein*, they benefited from the increased trade across the German Confederation. Austria was well aware of such developments and their implications. That is why it tried to develop an extended *Zollverein* to include Austria, those states still outwith the Prussian trade area, and indeed some states within it. As Andrina Stiles commented, 'The intentions were political rather than economic.'

Prussia, too, was well aware of the motives of Austria and instructed its representative at the *Bund*, Bismarck, to oppose such moves. In this, Prussia was successful.

> 66
>
> *Bismarck fought every inch of the way to prevent Austria from making the Zollverein an integral part of the constitution of the Confederation and thus gaining entry into it…*
>
> *The thrust of his endeavours always was not to allow Austria to enhance the importance of the Confederation in its own interests. It mattered little to him if in the process the concerns of Germany as a whole were neglected, provided those of Prussia were satisfied.*
>
> Edgar Feuchtwanger, Bismarck, 2002.

Evidence of the consequences of Austria's industrial backwardness was demonstrated to the world when its armies fared badly in the 1859 war with France and the Italian states. It was the chaos of Prussia's mobilisation during this war that was to precipitate the crisis over army reforms, and more specifically, how these were to be paid for, that would lead to the appointment of Bismarck as a 'last-chance' Prussian chancellor.

Source 4.4

This lithograph shows the battle at Montebello (20th May 1859) during the wars of Italian liberation and unification

Activity

This activity could involve the whole class, a small group or as few as two people. Use the format of a popular TV quiz. The structure of each quiz could be different and could provide increasing levels of difficulty as the quiz progresses.

All the participants should decide on the layout of the room, the amount of preparation, the prizes to be awarded and the pace and pressure for the contestants.

The Emergence of Bismarck

Introduction

The second half of the nineteenth century was the age of Bismarck. His skills, academic and diplomatic, were superior to all of his contemporaries, including Disraeli in Britain. There was hardly an event in Europe during this time that did not involve Bismarck. In the words of Ian Mitchell, 'Bismarck was everywhere'.

He was a man full of contradictions; having the narrow outlook of a Prussian *Junker*, he was to unify Germany under Prussian leadership. Politically he was very conservative but he helped to set up a form of late nineteenth- century welfare state. He was the man most associated with the policy of '*Eisen und Blut*' (Iron and Blood) to achieve his aims, yet he spent twenty years trying to keep Europe at peace. As German Chancellor he opposed becoming involved in a race to gain colonies yet he set up the German empire. In short, Bismarck dominated Europe, and to understand his actions helps to set our own world in context. The legacy of Bismarck along with the forces of liberalism, national-ism, socialism and, to a lesser degree, imperialism helped to create and continue to influence our understanding of today's world.

Bismarck's early life: 1815–1847

Otto von Bismarck was born in 1815, on the family estate at Schönhausen. His upbringing was typical of the son of a *Junker* family. Sent to boarding school in Berlin, he was a gifted foreign language student, speaking French, English and Russian in addition to his native tongue. In 1832, he went to Göttingen University and studied law, but spent many hours womanising, drinking and fighting duels.

At this time, he was not immune to the ideas of liberalism and nationalism but, in later life, he recanted.

Source 5.1

A young Otto von Bismarck

> *My historical sympathies remained on the side of authority. Yet my German National feeling remained so strong that, at the beginning of my university life, I at once entered into relations with the Burschenschaft, or group of students which made the promotion of national sentiment its aim. In my first half year at Göttingen occurred the Hambach Festival, the 'festal ode' of which still remains in my memory... but mob interference with political authority conflicted with my Prussian upbringing, and I returned to Berlin with less liberal opinions than when I quitted [left] it.*
>
> *Otto von Bismarck, Reflections and Reminiscences, 1899.*

In a recent biography of Bismarck, Edgar Feuchtwanger agrees with the above opinion.

> *Bismarck was convinced that German nationalism should not be a means of advancing the aims of the liberals, let alone democrats, it must be made subservient to the interests of the Prussian state.*
>
> *Edgar Feuchtwanger, Bismarck, 2002.*

When Bismarck graduated with a law degree in 1835 he was faced with a choice of equally unappealing careers – the army or the civil service. From 1835 to 1839, he worked at several civil service jobs but found the routine dull and uninteresting. It was during this time that he earned the nickname of the 'Mad *Junker*', spending much of his time drunk and chasing women. By 1847, he had little to show by way of personal achievement. On the other hand, as Andrina Stiles noted in *The Unification of Germany*, Bismarck had become ruthless, determined and unscrupulous in getting his own way. Such traits were to be illustrated when he was called into political service for the first time.

Bismarck's political life: 1847–1862

In 1847, the Prussian King, Frederick William IV, called a special meeting of the United *Diet* of the Prussian Estates. His aim was to raise money but he was so dissatisfied with the demands of this *Diet* that it was dissolved in December 1847. Bismarck had been elected as a member of this *Diet*, where he emerged as a defender of the rights of the monarchy. He enjoyed the cut and thrust of politics and his pro-monarchy stance had drawn him to the attention of the ultra-conservative groups around the king.

In 1848, with the outbreak of revolutionary unrest in Berlin, Bismarck was shocked by the concessions made to the revolutionaries by Frederick William IV and he argued that the king had lost the right to rule. He even

plotted to overthrow the monarch although these plans came to nothing. Bismarck was even more contemptuous of democracy and he became a firm believer in the use of force in politics to achieve ends. His regard for the king rose after Frederick William's refusal of the 'crown of shame' offered by the Frankfurt Assembly.

Later in the same year, much to Bismarck's delight, the liberal constitution granted in 1848 was abolished and replaced with a more conservative document, guaranteeing *Junker* dominance in Prussian politics. However, Bismarck was hostile to the proposed Erfurt Union and backed Prussia's climb-down in 1850, following acceptance of the Olmütz Pact. This restored the former *Bund* to its rightful place in German affairs.

Bismarck's conservative credentials made him attractive to the new Prussian chancellor, Manteuffel, and to the equally conservative Austrian chancellor, Schwarzenberg. His reward for opposition to the events of 1848–1849 was to be appointed in 1851 as Prussian representative to the restored *Bund*, meeting in Frankfurt. Here, he was initially supportive of Austrian proposals, but this had changed by 1854.

> "
> At Frankfurt, Bismarck was convinced that Austria and Prussia had to arrive at some definition of their respective spheres of influence in Central Europe.
>
> Edgar Feuchtwanger, Bismarck, 2002.

Source 5.2

Insulted by the behaviour of the Austrian delegate, Bismarck takes off his frock?

The first major confrontation with Austria occurred with the outbreak of the Crimean War in 1854. Austria called on the *Bund* to declare war on Russia in support of the British and French against Russia. Bismarck argued successfully that there would be no benefit for such a move for the *Bund*. Indeed, the only result would be the hatred of Russia and thus Bismarck advocated a policy of non-intervention.

> *No Prussian interests were affected in the meantime, and that if Austria's interests were endangered, it was not their duty to protect them; but on the contrary, that if Austria's position were weakened in a war, it would make Prussia's position in the Bund more potent [strong].*
>
> As quoted in Life of a Prince by William Jacks.

There can be little doubt that the Crimean War weakened Austria's international standing. Austria's half-hearted support of Britain and France earned little gratitude from them, while the failure to back Russia earned Austria the undying hostility of the Tsar.

In 1859, war broke out between Austria and France, which was helping Italy in its drive for national unity. Bismarck saw an opportunity to strike against Austria. Under the 1854 Treaty, Prussia was obliged to help Austria. With great reluctance, Prussia, now under the command of the Prince Regent (later King) William, who had replaced his insane brother Frederick William IV, mobilised its forces. The mobilisation was a shambles but Bismarck used the opportunity of Austrian distraction to urge an attack upon Prussia's southern rival.

> *The present situation has once again put the great prize in the lottery box for us if only we allow Austria's war against France to eat quite deeply at her substance. Then let us march southwards with our whole army with the boundary posts in the soldiers' knapsacks and drive them into the ground, either at Lake Constance or where Protestantism ceases to prevail.*
>
> Otto von Bismarck, 1859.

His suggested attack upon Austria was too much for the authorities to bear and he was removed from Frankfurt and sent as Ambassador to Saint Petersburg, Russia on 1 April 1859, where he remained for three years. Bismarck was welcomed in Russia and he soon realised that it was essential for the security of Prussia for his country to remain on friendly terms with Russia and he worked hard to maintain this all his working life.

In early 1862, he was sent to Paris as Ambassador to the court of Napoleon III. Bismarck soon realised that French power was more apparent than real. He was contemptuous of Napoleon III whom he

regarded as his intellectual inferior, and someone whom he could manipulate at his will. Nonetheless, he realised also that he required the friendship of France, at least initially, and this was easily accomplished as both had a mutual enemy in the form of Austria.

It was during this time in Paris that he decided to visit the International Exhibition being held in London. There he met one of Britain's leading Conservatives, Benjamin Disraeli and is reported to have commented on his plans for the future.

> "
> I [Bismarck] shall soon be compelled to undertake the conduct of the Prussian Government. As soon as the army shall have been brought into such a condition as to inspire respect, I shall seize the first best pretext to declare war against Austria, dissolve the German Diet and give national unity to Germany under Prussian leadership.
>
> Otto von Bismarck, 1862.

This has been seized upon by some historians to argue that Bismarck always did have a long-term plan for the unification of Germany. Others, like AJP Taylor, however, argued that Bismarck followed a day-to-day policy, taking the course most likely to achieve his aims.

It was events within Prussia itself that were to lead to his being summoned from Paris to become Prussian chancellor.

1862: The year of destiny

To understand why Bismarck was called upon to take up the highest office of state, we must reflect on a few events.

Frederick William IV was an unstable character who was declared insane in 1858. His brother, William, had served as an officer in the Prussian army and was a great believer in all things military. He was appointed Prince Regent in 1858 and after the disaster of Prussian mobilisation in 1859, he was convinced that thorough reform of the Prussian army was long overdue. As king, William, in discussion with the Minister of War, von Roon, proposed a series of reforms to restore Prussian military prestige. These included:

- a doubling in the size of the army
- an increased length of service from two to three years
- the abolition of the *Landwehr* (a sort of territorial army).

These proposals created a political storm in Berlin.

In 1859, the *Nationalverein* had been established with the aim of uniting Germany. It attracted much support from liberal, nationalist and middle-class groups and led to the formation of the Prussian Progressive Party. In the elections of 1862 to the Prussian *Diet*, this new party won a stunning victory, claiming 285 out of just over 300 seats available. In the aftermath of such a victory, the Prussian *Junkers* formed the Prussian Conservative Party to oppose any liberal and nationalist ideas.

One of the few powers granted to the *Diet* under the constitution of 1849 was control of the budget. Progressive Party opposition to the proposed reforms therefore centred on the battle to allow increased taxation to pay for the reforms. Although complaining of an increased tax burden which would fall on their supporters, the Progressives were also fearful that the abolition of the *Landwehr* would result in all organised military power being in the hands of the *Junker*-dominated army. To this end, the budget, and therefore the reforms, were rejected. Unfortunately, there appeared to be no clause in the constitution which could be used to resolve the conflict between king and parliament. His more conservative advisers suggested the setting up of a virtual military dictatorship but William feared that this would result in a bloodbath and rejected the idea. However, as no compromise seemed likely to suit both parties, William now thought of abdication. Such a move alarmed many of the king's ministers, who feared that this would result in the triumph of the elected body over the monarch.

It was in this tense situation that von Roon suggested to the king that Bismarck be recalled from Paris to help solve the dispute. Although reluctant to do so at first, the king eventually agreed and the now famous telegram, '*Periculum in mora, Depechez-vous!*' (Delay is dangerous. Hurry!) brought Bismarck to Berlin to take up the challenge of Prussian Chancellor.

Michael Gorman has argued that, at this stage, Bismarck's aims were to:

- resolve the constitutional crisis
- raise Prussia above Austria in German affairs
- create a greater role for Prussia in European affairs
- maintain the position of the *Junker* class.

His first task, though, was to solve the constitutional crisis – or he, too, might fall from power.

Bismarck's term in office saw the development of a new type of politics, referred to as *Realpolitik*. This was an emphasis on achieving realistic objectives, not pursuing idealistic ambitions.

The Emergence of Bismarck

> *Realpolitik meant that the age of ideology was ending and that politics would henceforth be dominated by material considerations and national interest rather than by abstract ideals.*
>
> Edgar Feuchtwanger, Bismarck, 2002.

Such an outlook led Bismarck to conclude that, while striving to maintain the position of the monarchy, it had to be accepted that unification was likely to happen at some stage. His aim was, therefore, to control the process and to see established a German nation where the power and position of the Prussian monarchy would be maintained. He was willing to risk the disruption of Austro-Prussian relations in order to achieve this end. He feared being swept away on a nationalist tide and he saw the best form of defence as attack. He made this clear in a speech to the Prussian *Diet*.

> *Germany does not look to Prussia's liberalism but to her power… Prussia must collect her forces and conserve them for an opportune moment which has already come and gone several times. Not by speeches and majorities will the great questions of the day be decided – that was the great mistake of 1848 and 1849 – but by iron and blood.*
>
> Otto von Bismarck, speech to the Prussian Diet,
> 30 September 1862.

Despite bullying and threats, the Progressives refused to give way. Bismarck then simply ignored the will of parliament and collected the taxes anyway. He claimed that there was no provision for the resolution of disputes between parliament and king. Because of this gap, the final decision rested with the king who resumed the right to carry on the government without parliamentary approval. Although objecting strongly to such an abuse of power and the trampling of the wishes of parliament, there was nothing that could be done as the king retained control of the armed forces.

Bismarck did realise that he could not continue to rule while he was permanently at war with the *Diet*. He sought some form of accommodation by pursuing their foreign policy interests while denying them any control of domestic affairs. In this he had several advantages. The king dared not dismiss Bismarck lest his own position be again threatened. There is no doubt that the army reforms had been effective and the quality of the Prussian army had been improved. Economically, Prussia was thriving due in part to the effects of the *Zollverein*. Finally, there had been a change in the relationships and roles of the Great Powers. Such conditions led Mosse to argue that Bismarck's success was not all of his own making.

> " Bismarck's task of unifying Germany was made easier by circumstances. If he played his hand with great skill, it was a good one in the first place.
>
> *Adapted from a speech by Gladstone, 1884.*

Bismarck's long-term aim was to unite Germany under Prussian leadership in the hope of eliminating domestic parliamentary opposition. After all, these Progressives were also fervent nationalists and they could hardly object to policies that would bring about the very thing they wanted – a united Germany. Thus, it was to the area of foreign affairs that Bismarck turned. Here he was able to exploit several circumstances to his, and Prussia's, advantage.

The Kingdom of Poland had been swallowed up by Russia, Austria and Prussia at the end of the eighteenth century. The Poles were desperate to re-establish their independence, and to that end there had been nationalist uprisings in 1830 and 1846, both ending in failure. In 1863, however, there was a large scale uprising in the Russian-occupied part of Poland. Fearing such a revolt might also spread to Prussian Poland, Bismarck saw advantages in joint action with the Russians. He instructed Alvensleben, Prussian Ambassador in Saint Petersburg, to reach an agreement with the Russians. The Alvensleben Convention allowed the Russian army to cross over the Prussian frontier in pursuit of Polish rebels. This agreement certainly assured Prussia of Russian gratitude. At the time Bismarck was criticised by Britain and France, both powers being sympathetic to the ideals of the Polish rebels. Ironically, this criticism helped Bismarck and Prussia as it convinced the Tsar of the hostility of the western powers towards Russia and that Prussia was the only friend his country had in Europe. Again Bismarck rode roughshod over opposition to the Convention in the Prussian *Diet*. It was affairs elsewhere in Europe that allowed him to fulfil the liberal nationalist ambitions of the Prussian Progressives.

Activity

Work in pairs or a group of three.

Design TWO word searches, each one no larger than 10 squares by 10 squares.

- One puzzle should contain words or phrases linked only to the main themes, issues or events developed in this chapter.

- The other puzzle could contain words or phrases linked only to the names of significant people or countries mentioned in this chapter.

- The words/phrases may be read vertically, horizontally or diagonally and forwards or backwards.

- Each word/phrase should have a clue to help identify it.

- When the word searches have been drafted, exchange them within the class.

A time limit could be set for completion of the puzzles.

Discuss any issues that arise from the activity.

6 The Wars of Unification

Introduction

By the 1860s, there were a number of forces at work which would improve the chances of Germany achieving unity, some internal and some external.

Within Germany, the idea of unity was gaining ground. In 1859, the German National Association was set up which, by 1862, had in excess of 25,000 members. More particularly, in Prussia, German liberals were prepared to end their calls for a constitutional form of government if these calls were a stumbling block to the achievement of unification. Prussia was also increasing in military, economic and financial strength – all vital ingredients if military action was being considered. The army appeared to be strong, with over 20% of the annual budget being spent on the armed forces. The railway network had increased by more than 100% since 1850. At the same time there was an increase in both coal and steel production. Prussia was also developing one of the best chemical industries in the world. Financially, the success of the *Zollverein* had provided the Prussian treasury with a large surplus.

Outside Germany, the success of Italian nationalists in the struggle to unite their states in the face of Austrian-backed opposition encouraged nationalists throughout Europe. Meanwhile, Austria was weakened as the result of a number of factors. Firstly, its failure to support Russia in the Crimean War of 1854–56 against Britain and France had cost Austria the friendship of Russia. Tsar Alexander II never forgave Austria for this betrayal. Economically, Austria was suffering due to its exclusion from the *Zollverein* and within its multi-ethnic empire, minorities were demanding civil rights and, in some cases, independence from Austria. There was also genuine sympathy for both the Italian and German struggles to achieve nationhood amongst the leading powers of Europe. Thus, Bismarck was operating in a much more favourable climate in the 1860s than his predecessors had faced in 1848–49. All he needed now was an opportunity to show the Liberals that he was in earnest in his claim to support their demands for unity, but on his terms. Prussia always came first, Germany second. He did not have to wait long.

The Danish War

The Danish crisis was to be a clear illustration of what became known as *Realpolitik* – the art of the possible, although not necessarily the desirable. Bismarck was not at all interested in the issues affecting two territories called Schleswig and Holstein but he saw the opportunity that the crisis created for him to exploit it for his own ends. As Edgar Feuchtwanger wryly commented, 'Bismarck was above all a Prussian'.

The history of the Danish problem was long and complicated, a comment from the British Prime Minister, Lord Palmerston, illustrating its difficulty. He stated, 'Only three men have ever understood it [the Danish crisis]. One was Prince Albert [husband of Queen Victoria] who is dead. The second was a German professor who went mad. I am the third and I have forgotten all about it.' However the issues can be briefly summarised as follows.

The Danish crisis arose over Schleswig and Holstein, two duchies on the border between Denmark and the German *Bund*, so called because they were under the supposed authority of a Duke.

In 1863 the new Danish King, Christian IX, decided to overturn the 1852 London Protocol, whereby Schleswig and Holstein were to be largely self-governing within the Danish kingdom. There was a large number of Danes living in North Schleswig, but the rest of the population of the two duchies of Schleswig and Holstein were mostly German in origin. Holstein was a member of the German *Bund*, but Schleswig was not.

Bismarck realised that the German nationalists were outraged at the idea of the loss of Holstein as a member of the *Bund*. By taking action, he could portray himself and Prussia as a defender of German nationalism. Such an intervention would also, coincidentally, prove to the Prussian Parliament that the army reforms they so bitterly opposed had indeed been worthwhile. But Bismarck had to be careful. An earlier Danish attempt to annex (take over) Schleswig and Holstein in 1848 had resulted in Prussia acting alone but later being forced to back down by Austria. Bismarck did not want a repeat of this outcome so he had to convince Austria that it should join with Prussia in acting against the threat posed by the Danish demands. In addition, by taking the lead in defending the two duchies, Bismarck showed that Prussia was more interested in defending German interests than Austria was. This was why Bismarck formed an alliance with Austria in late 1863 to defend the position of the duchies within the Danish kingdom.

Another characteristic of Bismarck's policy can be identified in the coming war. He always ensured that his enemy was isolated, with no hope of foreign assistance. This was achieved in 1864 as a result of a range of circumstances.

Britain was not in a position to help as it was first and foremost a naval power. Any help for the Danes would require the assistance of a major European land power and Britain wanted to avoid such entanglements. Additionally, Queen Victoria was sympathetic to the cause of German unity, especially so since the death of her husband, Prince Albert (himself a German) in 1861.

France was in no position to offer help as it was involved in a foreign adventure in Mexico at this time. Russia, too, was indifferent. As a result of the Alvensleben Convention (see Chapter 5, page 45) the Tsar considered Bismarck as a friend.

Thus, the scene was set. Denmark, in clear breach of the London Protocol of 1852, found itself isolated, facing the combined forces of Prussia and Austria.

The war began on 1 February 1864. Denmark was quickly overwhelmed by its enemies and entered into negotiations in April. Hoping for European support, the Danes dragged their heels until, in August, the war was renewed and the Danes were compelled to submit by the Treaty of Vienna. In this the Danish King abandoned all claims to the duchies and at the same time, joint rule (the term used to describe this is a condominium) was established over the two duchies by Prussia and Austria.

Debate over the role of Bismarck in this war continues.

> **"**
>
> *When the Schleswig-Holstein affair arose again, Bismarck intervened because he had to… It is clear that Bismarck wanted the question settled in the interests of Prussia.*
>
> LCB Seaman.

> **"**
>
> *He [Bismarck] set the diplomatic challenge [to Austria] by skilful manipulation of a dispute between the Bund and Denmark. Prussia's intervention would indicate future leadership and raise Prussia's prestige.*
>
> David Thomson, Europe since Napoleon, 1965.

One of Bismarck's contemporaries, Frederick Engels, pointed out that there was a difference in results and methods.

> **"**
>
> *In the matter of the Duchies, Bismarck had fulfilled the wishes of the bourgeoisie against their will. The fulfilment of national aspirations of the bourgeoisie was well under way, but the method chosen was not liberal.*
>
> Frederick Engels.

The Austro–Prussian War

Having dealt with the Danes, Bismarck now turned his attention to his great rival, Austria. He would have to expel Austria from the *Bund* if his aim of unification of Germany under Prussian leadership was to be achieved. Cameron, Robertson and Henderson are of the opinion that he had planned for this.

> "
>
> *There is absolutely no doubt that he [Bismarck] set his sights on Austria once the crisis [Schleswig-Holstein] had passed over and worked to isolate her from the other European powers.*

David Thomson would agree with this point of view, stating that, 'There is no doubt that Bismarck wanted and planned for war against Austria.'

As before, Bismarck set about isolating his future enemy and destroying any support Austria might have amongst potential allies. However, war nearly came before he was ready.

After the ending of the Danish war, joint rule had been established in the duchies. Whether Bismarck had intended this to fail is not clear. What is clear is that the two powers had very different ideas as to how the areas should be ruled. Bismarck was keen to annex the two territories, while Austria argued that their fate should be decided by the *Bund*. Belatedly the Austrians realised that they had been dragged into a war from which they were to receive no real benefits. Talk of war between the two powers grew louder.

At this stage, Bismarck was not yet ready for war. His diplomatic and military preparations were incomplete and he had to play for time. In August 1865, the two powers patched up their differences by the Convention of Gastein. The terms were that Prussia should rule Schleswig and Austria should rule Holstein.

Ian Mitchell has described this convention as a 'master-stroke' since it appeared that Austria had been outmanoeuvred by Bismarck; a quarrel could be chosen at any time suitable to Bismarck over the administration of the area, and to the smaller southern German states it appeared that Austria was only interested in acquiring more land for its empire. Crucially, Prussia now controlled Austrian access to its duchy, since Holstein was now surrounded by Prussian territory.

Now Bismarck could turn his attention to completing his war preparations. In a series of diplomatic moves, he isolated Austria prior to the outbreak of hostilities.

France had to be persuaded to remain neutral in any such Austro–Prussian war. Bismarck played on the belief of Napoleon III that the German states should continue to be divided. He was also aware of the French emperor's desire to expand the territorial limits of France, and indeed to undo the terms of the Vienna Settlement of 1815. Therefore, if Bismarck wanted to reshape the balance of power in Europe, he would need to offer the French something in return for its neutrality.

To this end, in October 1865, Bismarck 'happened' to meet Napoleon III at the resort of Biarritz. No record of their meeting was kept and historians can speculate about what was agreed by retracing events from the war of 1866 and its aftermath. It would appear that Napoleon was convinced that if France were to remain neutral in any war between Prussia and Austria, France would be granted territorial compensation 'wherever French is spoken'. This certainly seemed to Napoleon to include Belgium and even parts of the west bank of the Rhine.

Source 6.1

Bismarck and Napoleon III on the beach of Biarritz 1863

It was fairly safe to assume that Britain would not intervene. After all, it had not done so in 1864 and little had changed since then as far as Britain was concerned. Russia, too, could be counted on to remain neutral at the very least, as the Tsar was still grateful to Bismarck over Poland and he had never forgiven Austria for failing to support Russia in the Crimean War of 1854–1856.

Bismarck was also keen to have an ally in Europe, to prevent the image of a civil war between the two German powers attracting the interest of the other European nations. He settled on Italy for a variety of reasons. Firstly, the Italians regarded Austria as a stumbling block to the creation of a fully-united Italy, since the Austrians still occupied the area of Venetia. Secondly, in any war between Austria and Prussia and Italy, the Austrians would be at the military disadvantage of having to fight a war on two fronts.

Nonetheless, the Italians drove a hard bargain. Victor Emmanuel II of Italy did not really trust Bismarck and did not want to be left in the lurch if and

when it suited Bismarck. So he insisted upon the following conditions for the proposed Prussian–Italian alliance:

- the alliance would last only three months
- Austria had to declare war
- Italy would declare war after Prussia
- Italy would obtain Venetia as a reward.

The issue now facing Bismarck was how to force conflict with Austria within the three-month window of opportunity the Italian alliance had given him.

To this end, he began to increase pressure on Austria by declaring that elections to the *Bund* should be by universal male suffrage. This was totally unacceptable to all the other German states. However, before thinking that Bismarck had been transformed into a liberal, it is necessary to note that once the offer was made, it was left to the other German states to respond. Their rejection of the proposal, a proposal welcomed by the liberals, made them appear to be the reactionaries, while Bismarck could portray himself in a liberal light. This was just another example of his manipulation of political means for his own ends. After all, he had been at war with the liberals in Prussia since coming to power over the issue of the army budget. Here, he was again using events to try to score points and curry favour with the liberals at home.

But Bismarck was also still faced with the need to force Austria to declare war if his Italian alliance was to hold. Fortunately, the actions of the Austrians helped Bismarck's cause. He was able to rouse Austrian anger over the issue of the latter's access to Holstein. Knowing that its army was inferior to that of their enemy, the Austrians had no option but to begin the mobilisation of its army ahead of Prussia. This was partly in response to Italian troop movements near Austria's southern frontier in late April 1866. Bismarck used this as an excuse to bully the Prussian king into mobilising Prussian forces. To the rest of Europe, the stationing of Austrian troops on Prussia's frontier gave the impression that Austria was the aggressor, and this meant Austria would receive no sympathy from them. In fact, Austria was so isolated in Europe that when the other European powers proposed a conference to avert war, the Austrians refused to attend. Bismarck, despite the upset that it might cause to his Italian alliance, had accepted. Thus, it seemed to Europe that it was Austria who was responsible for the war.

Austria decided to take the initiative, ended talks over Schleswig and Holstein and instead proposed that the matter should be decided by the *Bund*. This was against the terms of the Gastein Convention and Bismarck now ordered the Prussian army to invade Holstein on 10 June 1866. Bismarck now raised the tension even more by proposing on 10 June the creation of a new German state, excluding Austria, and calling for elections to a national assembly to create it. This was the final straw and

on 14 June 1866, Austria declared war on Prussia. All of Bismarck's carefully laid plans could now come into effect. Bismarck also issued ultimata to Saxony, Hanover, Bavaria, Württemberg and Baden to join with Prussia or be considered enemies. They all sided with Austria, as expected, and with their rejection of Bismarck's demands, the Austro–Prussian war began.

With the outbreak of war, Bismarck was careful to keep German nationalists 'on side'. Part of the declaration of war on Austria included a call to all Germans.

> " Let the German people come forward in confidence to meet Prussia. Let it help to promote and make secure the peaceful development of our common Fatherland.
>
> *Prussian Declaration of War, 1866.*

Thus, Bismarck was able to portray Prussia as fighting to establish a modern unified German state.

Hesse and Saxony were immediately invaded by Prussia once war began and neither offered any resistance. By the end of June, the Hanoverian resistance had collapsed. In the South, the Italians were badly mauled by the Austrians but this was largely irrelevant to the conduct of the war. They achieved no more and no less than Bismarck had expected, keeping 200,000 Austrian troops involved in the area. This greatly helped the Prussians at the only major battle of the war, the Battle of Königgrätz (or Sadowa) on 3 July 1866.

Source 6.2

Austro-Prussian War 1866. Battle of Königgrätz on 3rd July 1866.

The Wars of Unification

The war was a stunning success for Prussia. It had been assumed that the two sides were evenly matched. Indeed, Napoleon III considered this to be the case, reckoning that the war would be long and fought out to a stalemate, enabling him to step in and act as arbitrator. How wrong he and the rest of Europe were. Prussian superiority over Austria bore fruit. Using its extensive rail network, the Prussians were able to move large forces relatively quickly to the battlefront. The telegraph was used to enable Prussian generals to communicate directly back to Berlin. Despite superior Austrian artillery, the Prussian army was better organised, had better rifles and used superior tactics in combat.

After sustaining large casualties, and with no Austrian army between the Prussians and Vienna, the Austrians accepted overwhelming defeat.

Bismarck now wanted to end the war quickly and was prepared to offer the Austrians generous terms . He argued that, 'We have to avoid wounding too severely.' Bismarck had achieved his aim of pushing the Austrians out of German affairs. He also feared a severe Italian defeat and there was always the possibility of French intervention. So, despite opposition from both King William I (overcome by the now well-rehearsed threat to resign) and the Prussian generals, Bismarck ended the war. An armistice was signed at Nikolsburg on 26 July 1866 and the war was formally concluded by the Treaty of Prague of 23 August 1866.

The terms of the treaty were beneficial to Prussia but were also accepted by Austria as generous.

- Austria gave up the territory around Venice called Venetia which was transferred to the Italian kingdom
- Austria was expelled from the *Bund* but would lose no land and only had to pay a small amount of compensation
- Schleswig, Holstein, Hesse-Cassel, Frankfurt and Hanover were all taken over by Prussia
- the 21 states north of the river Main were to form a North German Confederation under Prussian leadership
- the southern German states were to remain independent, but were forced to pay large indemnities to Prussia
- the southern German states were also forced into military alliances with Prussia.

The results of the war were spectacular. Despite Austria's defeat, it was soon able to re-establish good relations with Prussia. French power and prestige had been reduced. At home, Bismarck was now regarded as a national hero. Even the liberals forgave him for his unconstitutional rule of Prussia from 1862 by passing an indemnity act giving retrospective approval for his actions and voted him a reward of £60,000.

Feuchtwanger has viewed this as a major departure in Bismarck's career.

> It was the turning point when Bismarck ceased to be a gambler living precariously and became the towering, overwhelming figure that dominated Germany and Europe for the next twenty five years.
>
> *Edgar Feuchtwanger, Bismarck, 2002.*

The origins of the Franco–Prussian War

Although he was acclaimed by many German nationalists as a hero, Bismarck was well aware that their aims had not yet been fully satisfied. The states north of the River Main were united in the North German Confederation, but the position of the southern German states had still to be settled. One solution would have been for Prussia simply to have annexed these to the Confederation. However, this would have exacerbated the suspicion between north and south over the issue of religion and Prussian domination and the result would have been nothing but hatred towards Prussia. He slowly came round to the idea that the southern German opposition could only be overcome by creating an enemy who was even more dangerous to the South German states than Prussia.

> I [Bismarck] assumed that a united Germany was only a question of time, that the North German Confederation was only the first step in its solution. I did not doubt that a Franco–Prussian War must take place before the construction of a united Germany could be realised. I was at that time preoccupied with the idea of delaying the outbreak of war until our military strength should be increased.
>
> *Otto von Bismarck, Reflections and Reminiscences, 1898.*

Historians have used this to argue that Bismarck deliberately set out on a plan of war with France. However, debate continues to rage over Bismarck's actions. Gorman argues that 'war was not his sole aim, but it was one of a variety of possibilities open to him.' Williamson would agree with this to an extent.

> Bismarck knowingly risked war, even though he probably hoped to avoid it, as there appeared no other way of accelerating the unification of Germany.
>
> *DG Williamson, Bismarck and Germany, 1986.*

A different stance is taken by Mitchell who notes 'almost as soon as Bismarck had dealt with Austria, there began the conflict with Napoleon

III which was to lead to the Franco–Prussian war of 1870–1871. David Thomson points out that 'from 1866 onward, relations between France and Germany remained tense' and describes Bismarck as a man using 'unscrupulous tactics' in his dealings with the French.

There were several issues creating tension between France and Prussia, the first being Napoleon III's belief that he should be rewarded for remaining neutral in the Austro–Prussian war. Bismarck rejected Napoleon's demands but asked for them to be put in writing 'for future consideration', which the French emperor was happy to do. These demands were then promptly leaked to the press, causing fury amongst the southern German states as much of the compensation was to be taken from their lands. Thus, reluctantly, the southern German states were drawn into Prussia's orbit through the need for a powerful 'big brother' to oppose the French bully. This fear of French expansionism had played into Bismarck's hands.

Bismarck also seemed to encourage, or even manoeuvre, Napoleon III in his ambitions to increase his influence, once over Luxembourg and once concerning Belgium. On both those issues Bismarck must have known the rest of Europe, and especially Britain, would be unhappy about French actions. On both occasions Napoleon III had to climb down. Certainly relations between France and Prussia were chilly by the end of the 1860s and by that time the need to prevent further Prussian expansion became a priority for Napoleon III. It was unlikely that the creation of a united Germany could be achieved without war, yet from Bismarck's viewpoint he still required an excuse for war, a way of isolating France and a means of entrapment of the southern German states through military alliances, economic ties and bribery. Such an opportunity arose in Spain.

The Spanish Candidature is a classic example of how Bismarck used a situation, not of his own creating, to advance his own aims. As McKichan wrote, 'in 1870, Bismarck was clearly using the question of the Spanish throne to stir up trouble with France.'

> "
> It seems certain that Bismarck engineered the dispute [between France and Prussia] by supporting the Hohenzollern candidate for the Spanish crown. Bismarck wanted war. He believed that the time was ripe.
>
> David Thomson, Europe since Napoleon, 1965.

What was the Spanish Candidature?

The Spanish Parliament was seeking to appoint a new king, following the removal of Queen Isabella. Bismarck saw a further chance to antagonise

Germany 1815–1939

France by placing a Prussian prince on the throne of Spain, thereby encircling France. He knew that France would never accept such a proposal, since this threatened its security. The Prussian king, William I, was also reluctant, fearing it might lead to war with France. Bismarck bullied him into nominating a minor member of the Hohenzollern royal family, Prince Leopold, as Prussia's nominee.

Bismarck had hoped to have the deal signed before the French found out about his scheme. However, France did find out and was enraged. The French ambassador to Prussia, Benedetti, was instructed to demand the withdrawal of Leopold, or Prussia would face war.

King William had always been against the candidature and he pressured Leopold into withdrawing. When news of this reached Bismarck, he was appalled at the king's actions and even thought of resignation.

Source 6.3

Telegraph from 1870 about the meeting between William I of Prussia and the French ambassador Benedetti; edited by Bismarck it resulted in the French declaration of war against Germany.

Napoleon III now saw the chance to exact revenge on Prussia in general, and Bismarck in particular, for all of the previous humiliations. Benedetti was again instructed to demand that the Hohenzollern candidature would never be renewed. Breaking diplomatic protocol, he approached the Prussian king on the street in the town of Bad Ems. William told Benedetti that he could not make such a guarantee about future actions. He then sent a telegram to his chancellor, detailing French demands and a summary of what had taken place.

Bismarck saw the potential for action. Editing what became known as 'the Ems Telegram', he altered its tone, making the meeting at Ems seem like a snub to the French. The edited text was released to the press.

The French politicians were incensed at this version of events. They demanded that the emperor declare war on Prussia, an action he reluctantly agreed to on 19 July 1870. This allowed Bismarck, once more, to pose as the innocent victim of French aggression.

The Wars of Unification

Historians have clear views on Bismarck's actions. Seaman believed that:

> *The action of Bismarck [editing and releasing the Ems telegram] was his own free choice and he must bear responsibility… Bismarck could have done little had not his victims made themselves his accomplices [helpers] by their folly [foolishness].*

Feuchtwanger summed up the situation neatly when he wrote, 'A war with France breaking out under the right circumstances might well be the catalyst for bringing the South German states to the side of Prussia.'

Bismarck had ensured French isolation by publishing French plans for compensation in the southern German states. Alarmed by the possible French threat, the military alliances with the southern German states came into effect and all decided that they would have to back Prussia in a war of national defence against France.

The outcome of the Franco–Prussian War

Once again Prussian military and economic strength was decisive. The French army was defeated at Worth in August 1870, and again at Sedan, in the following month. The fleeing army was besieged in Metz, and Paris was besieged and fell in January 1871. The Emperor, Napoleon III was captured and a republic was declared. Finally, on 18 January 1871 in the Hall of Mirrors in the Palace of Versailles William I, King of Prussia, was proclaimed German Emperor.

The peace treaty which followed the war was very different to the one with Austria. The Treaty of Frankfurt, made in May 1871, was a harsh, punitive treaty and Cameron, Henderson and Robertson are of the view that the Treaty of Frankfurt represented a cruel, victor's peace. This was partly due to the desire of William to annex territory (something which Bismarck had not allowed in 1866) and also to the military that insisted upon annexation as a way of defending the new German states from a vengeful France. The result was a treaty that no French government could support.

For example, Metz and Strasbourg were annexed to Germany and France had to pay an indemnity (compensation) of £200,000,000 within four years. But it was the fate of Alsace and Lorraine that was to create a festering sore in French–German relations until 1914 provided the opportunity for French revenge. LCB Seaman commented that, 'A France deprived of Alsace–Lorraine by war guaranteed the insecurity of Germany, while DG Williamson added, 'In retrospect few would disagree that this [annexation of Alsace–Lorraine] was a miscalculation of great consequence.'

Source 6.4

1 September 1870 – Napoleon III and Bismarck on the morning after the battle of Sedan

How important was Bismarck to German unification?

There are differing views on the overall importance of Bismarck to unification.

Until the mid-twentieth century, it was generally accepted that Bismarck alone was responsible for the unification of Germany under Prussian domination. Otto Pflanze wrote that, 'only under the stimulation provided by Bismarck for his own political ends did German nationalism begin to move the masses. This view was perpetuated, even by Hitler, who commented that, 'it was he [Bismarck] who created the conditions which rendered possible the creation of Great Germany.'

However, since that time, the interaction of other factors has been considered. Williamson argued that, 'Bismarck did not fashion German unity alone. He exploited powerful forces which already existed – economic, liberalism and nationalism.' Mosse would contend that 'Bismarck's task of unifying Germany was made easier by circumstances', while Medlicott noted that, 'His [Bismarck's] admirers often exaggerate the extent of the obstacles in his path.' Aronson believed that Bismarck was an opportunist and Stiles thought that 'his policies can best be described as flexible'.

Other later writers have taken a stance more hostile to Bismarck. The German historian Eric Eyck has argued that, 'German unification in the third quarter of the nineteenth century was a natural and desirable development' while others would emphasise the economic dominance of Prussia as a natural lead to political unification – what Seaman would refer to as 'coal and iron', rather than 'iron and blood'.

Activity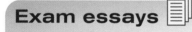

1 Re-read the chapter carefully.

2 Make two lists, the first showing the actions of Bismarck **which led to German unification** and the second listing the actions of others.

3 Use the evidence from the list to reach conclusions about the role played by each in the unification of Germany. Present your views about which of these was more important and provide relevant evidence to support your opinion.

Review Activity

Devise and draw a cartoon that sums up Bismarck's role in unification.

It should show Bismarck's role but also try to show the other elements that combined to assist him in his creation of a united Germany.

Exam essays

1 How important was Bismarck to German unification?

2 Without Prussian military power Germany would not have become united in 1871. Do you agree?

7 Bismarck's Reich

Introduction

On 18 January 1871, in the Hall of Mirrors in the Palace of Versailles near Paris, Bismarck had the honour of proclaiming the birth of the German Empire. In the minds of both Germans and French, the founding of the empire would, forever, be associated with a military triumph for Germany and a humiliating defeat for France. The occasion should have been the culmination of Bismarck's career to date but the reality was much more mundane. Bismarck and his monarch had fallen out over the exact nature of the title to be conferred on William I. The king favoured the title of Emperor of Germany. Bismarck, aware of the sensitivities of the other German kings and princes, suggested the compromise of German Emperor. To avoid a repetition of the fiasco of the offer of the crown of a united Germany to Frederick William IV in 1849, Bismarck had even bribed King Ludwig II of Bavaria into sending a letter offering William the crown of a united country. The other princes and rulers were persuaded to add their signatures. Thus, it appeared that it was his fellow rulers who were proclaiming William emperor.

Source 7.1

Founding of the German Empire on 18 January 1871. King William I of Prussia is proclaimed German Emperor in the Hall of Mirrors at The Palace of Versailles.

7

The birth of the German Empire

There were other significant factors to be taken into account. The new empire was a far cry from the ideal envisaged by the revolutionaries of 1848–1849. Firstly, it contained significant numbers of foreigners such as Poles in the eastern Prussian lands, Danes in Schleswig and Frenchmen in Alsace and Lorraine. Secondly, the empire left significant numbers of Germans excluded from the new Reich, most notably in lands occupied by Austria–Hungary (Austria became Austria–Hungary in 1867). Thirdly, with Prussia having 60% of the land and 60% of the population, the new empire was more an extension than a unification. Prussia would dominate the new country. This is best illustrated by the fact that, when a common currency was adopted, it was the Prussian one which was extended throughout the country. Similarly, the new legal system was based on the Prussian model and it was the Prussian bank which became the Reichsbank. In fact it could be argued that rather than having been unified the Germany states had been Prussianised.

The Constitution became law on 20 April 1871 and it, too, mirrored the Prussification of Germany. The King of Prussia was automatically also German Emperor with extensive powers over the armed forces, the civil service and the foreign policy of the new Reich. The Prussian Chancellor automatically became Chancellor of Germany and between 1871 and 1890 that was Bismarck. He was appointed by, and responsible to, only

Source 7.2

New German Empire after 1871

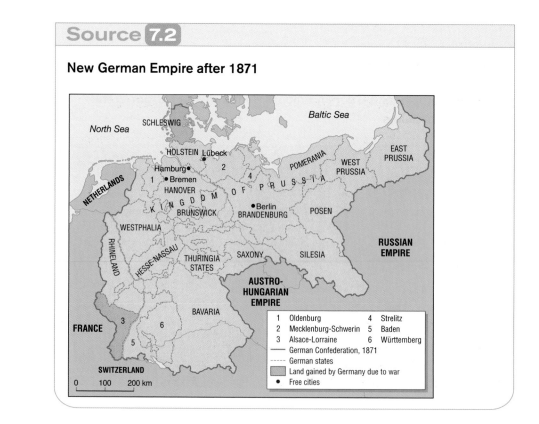

1	Oldenburg	4	Strelitz
2	Mecklenburg-Schwerin	5	Baden
3	Alsace-Lorraine	6	Württemberg

— German Confederation, 1871
---- German states
▓ Land gained by Germany due to war
• Free cities

the emperor. He also chaired the meetings of the *Bundesrat* (see below) which meant that he had a virtual stranglehold on the apparatus of the new government.

DG Williamson comments that, until his resignation in 1890, Bismarck dominated the Reich government. This was due largely to the huge influence Bismarck had over the emperor – and the confidence the emperor had in Bismarck. Contemporaries were also aware of the power and influence of Bismarck. Lady Emily Russell, wife of the British ambassador, commented on this in 1880.

> "
> *The emperor has allowed Prince Bismarck to have his own way in everything; and the great chancellor revels in the absolute power he has acquired and does as he pleases.*
>
> Lady Emily Russell, 1880.

As long as William I lived, Bismarck was secure. But what would happen if the emperor changed?

> "
> *By force of personality and influence, he [Bismarck] was able to hold the federal structure together, but the danger remained that under a different monarch and a different chancellor, the old disunity would reassert itself.*
>
> DG Williamson, Bismarck and Germany, 1986.

The powers given to the emperor were virtually under Bismarck's control until 1890 but when William II became emperor in 1888 a clash between emperor and chancellor became almost inevitable.

The composition of the Empire

There were two parts to the new German government – the *Bundesrat* and the *Reichstag*.

The *Bundesrat* was made up of 58 appointed representatives of the 25 states which comprised the new Germany. Its purpose was to make new laws and it had the right to declare war. However, if Germany were attacked, that right was in the hands of the emperor. The number of representatives was based in proportion to the size of the state's population. Thus, Prussia had 17 seats. Compared to the total of 58 it would appear at first glance that Prussian influence was restricted but as only 14 votes were needed to block any legislation, Prussia maintained a stranglehold over the *Bundesrat*. Indeed, it never voted against the wishes of Prussia. The *Bundesrat* was also chaired by the imperial chancellor and Bismarck controlled and manipulated the *Bundesrat* for his own ends up until 1890.

The *Reichstag* contained 382 members, elected by all men over the age of twenty five. However the powers of the *Reichstag* were very limited. Although it could question the chancellor it could not dismiss him nor create new laws. Thus its power was largely illusionary. Andrina Stiles has argued in *The Unification of Germany* that Bismarck was contemptuous of the *Reichstag*, viewing it as nothing more than a meeting house for squabbling politicians who did not represent popular public opinion.

Finlay McKichan, too, has questioned the value of such a constitution, arguing that it was a façade behind which Bismarck hid his contempt for democracy. Certainly, the constitution gave little chance for democracy, in its true sense, to be exercised and this was reinforced by the prominent role that the army was to play in German politics until 1945. The army had helped the birth of the new country and generals continued to influence government policy without being accountable to the electorate. This is why certain historians have concluded that the constitution of 1871 was authoritarian rather than democratic.

On the other hand, it has to be recognised that all men over 25 could vote long before the same was true in Britain, a free press existed and there was political choice with a range of different political parties. Also, *Reichstag* representatives did influence crucial decisions. To dismiss the *Reichstag* out of hand would be a mistake as even Bismarck spent long hours trying to ensure support for his policies in the *Reichstag*. Overall it is hard to disagree with the views of Grant and Temperley.

Source 7.3

This cartoon from 1878 reads: 'How the future Reichstag will look when ... the Chancellor is able to assemble a contingent of enough 'close personal associates'.

> "
> *Bismarck had thus settled the internal Government of Germany by supplying it with an upper house representing states, a pseudo-democratic lower house representing numbers; with a constitution excluding many matters from the (control) of both bodies and which could not be amended without Prussian permission. Prussia through her prestige, her money, her power was emphatically the predominant power.*
>
> AJ Grant and Harold Temperley, Europe in the 19th and 20th Centuries, 1952.

Gründungszeit

The decade of the 1870s is often referred to by German historians as '*Gründungszeit*' (Foundation Time). It was during this period that the main German political parties emerged with their agendas for the new empire. A brief look at each of these parties and their demands will provide an insight into their importance in German political life.

- The **Conservatives** were made up mostly of Protestant Prussian landowners. They were on the extreme right of party politics and opposed any liberal measure. At the same time they remained suspicious of Bismarck's policies and considered many of them to be dangerous.
- The **Free Conservatives** were supported by landowners and industrialists throughout Germany. They tended to back Bismarck unquestioningly.
- The **National Liberals** drew their support predominantly from the middle classes. They were keen to see the economic development of Germany continue and were supporters of free trade policies.
- The **Progressives** had split from the National Liberals in 1867 over the pardon given to Bismarck for his unconstitutional rule in Prussia from 1862. Although supportive of most of the policies of the National Liberals, they were bitterly hostile towards Bismarck.
- The **Centre (*Zentrum*) Party** was formed to defend the interests of the Roman Catholic minority within the new Protestant Germany. Initially hostile to Bismarck, they became some of his staunchest supporters after 1879.
- The **Social Democrats** won most of their support from the industrial areas of Germany. They grew more powerful after a merger of two main socialist groups in 1875. They remained hostile to Bismarck throughout his long period in office.

The decade of the 1870s is also known as the Liberal Era. During this time, Bismarck did not belong to any political party nor did he consistently support any one political policy. In fact it can be said he applied *realpolitik* to his domestic as well as foreign policies.

At first Bismarck worked with the National Liberals, the majority party in the *Reichstag* in the early 1870s, to pass legislation broadly favourable to the development of commerce and industry, including a policy of free trade. The two had much in common. The National Liberals had favoured the creation of a united Germany and the 1871 constitution while Bismarck relied on this group during the period of the *Kulturkampf* (Struggle for Civilisation).

What was the *Kulturkampf*?

The term *Kulturkampf* was coined by a left-liberal Reichstag deputy, Rudolf Virchow.

> "
> *The struggle against the Roman Catholic Church was, with every day that passed, acquiring more and more the character of a great struggle for civilisation [Kulturkampf] in the interests of humanity.*
>
> Rudolf Virchow, speech to the Reichstag, 1872.

Having created the German Empire, like any other parent, Bismarck now sought to protect his 'child' from forces whom he considered hostile to it. He was always suspicious of minorities and saw plots and revolution everywhere. One such group was the Roman Catholic minority within Germany. By excluding Austria–Hungary from the new Reich by his *kleindeutsch* solution, Bismarck ensured that the Roman Catholics in southern Germany now found themselves without a protector against Protestant Prussia. The Catholic minority (but still making up over 35% of the total Reich population) felt obliged to organise politically in order to defend their interests. Early in 1871, the Centre Party was formed to defend the rights of Germany's Catholics, to oppose religious oppression and to demand state aid for the poor of Germany. To make matters worse in the eyes of Bismarck, this new party became the focus for many individuals and groups opposed to him. The Centre Party (*Zentrum*) also attracted support from the French living in Alsace and Lorraine and the Poles living in the eastern parts of Prussia. Bismarck viewed all of these as forces of disunity (he used the term *Reichsfeinden* – enemies of the empire – to describe them) within the new country and, by attacking them, he hoped to weaken any forces working for the destruction of the empire. His view was confirmed in the 1871 Reichstag elections when the Centre Party won 57 seats, reinforcing Bismarck's view that the party would encourage civil disobedience when and where state politics conflicted with their religious convictions. Bismarck had other worries about the Centre Party. Firstly, he feared its loyalty would lie with the Pope in Rome and not with Germany. Secondly, in the wars of unification he had defeated the Catholic powers of France and Austria–Hungary, both powers regarded favourably by the *Zentrum*.

Despite this, however, it would be wrong to see this *Kulturkampf*, or 'Struggle for Civilisation', as a religious struggle. Bismarck always viewed it as a political contest.

> *For Bismarck the Kulturkampf was a fight against forces hostile to the state, namely to himself, and would eventually end when it was no longer required.*
>
> Rudolf Virchow, speech to the Reichstag, 1872.

And as DG Williamson noted, 'Bismarck did exploit the political advantages afforded by the *Kulturkampf* for his own ends.'

Certainly it is clear that Bismarck did see the political opportunities provided by the campaign as a means to strengthen his alliance with the National Liberals who were increasingly concerned by rather authoritarian pronouncements from the Pope, particularly the Doctrine of Papal Infallibility which in 1870 had confirmed that in the area of faith and morals, the Pope could not be wrong.

Source 7.4

Infallible and Unfellable – Caricature of the dogma of infallibility granted to the Pope at the Vatican Council sitting of 18th July 1870.

Unfehlbar und Unfällbar.

The effects of *Kulturkampf*

The attack began with the publication of a series of violently anti-Catholic newspaper articles. This was followed, in 1871, with the abolition of the Roman Catholic section of the Prussian Ministry of Religion and Education. The following year the rights of Roman Catholics to supervise their faith schools were abolished. In the same year, Jesuits, the 'soldiers' of Christ, were expelled from Germany. But the real blow came in 1873 with the adoption of the 'May Laws' of Adalbert Falk, the Prussian Minister of Religion and Education. He had been appointed with instructions from Bismarck, 'to re-establish the rights of the church vis-à-vis the state'.

Amongst other terms, Falk's laws brought the Catholic Church more fully under central control by state supervision of their schools, forbidding priests to conduct religious services unless they had been trained in Germany, banning the appointment of clergy by the state and imposing a reduction in state financial aid to the Catholic Church. Additionally, all religious orders were abolished with the exception of those working in the medical field, and civil marriages became compulsory. Within Prussia, Roman Catholics lost some civil and legal rights.

The result was the opposite of what Bismarck had intended. Far from weakening the Centre Party, it flourished under Bismarck's persecution. In the 1874 elections, the Centre Party increased its representation from 57 to 91 seats and to 93 in 1877. Outwith Germany, the Pope ordered the Catholic bishops to urge ordinary Catholics to disobey any anti-Catholic laws, but Bismarck countered by forbidding the bishops from publishing the Pope's letter. The result was stalemate. Despite papal attempts at reconciliation, even the emperor was to write that there was a real split.

> "
> To my deep sorrow, a portion of my Catholic subjects have organised over the space of two years a political party which has sought to disturb, by intrigues hostile to the state, the religious peace which has existed in Prussia for centuries.
>
> Emperor William I, 1877.

As long as Pius IX lived and Bismarck was in power there was no chance of a compromise. However, events were developing both at home and abroad which made the ending of the *Kulturkampf* politically essential for Bismarck.

In 1873, Germany suffered an economic collapse and this was followed by a lengthy depression. The National Liberals, as champions of the doctrine of free trade, were blamed for this collapse. Industry and landowners demanded that Germany impose tariffs on foreign goods entering the

country. The farming crisis forced the Conservative Party to demand protection for German farmers and the Centre Party, under pressure from its own farmer and craftsmen supporters, wanted the same. By now Bismarck also favoured a policy of tariffs since a number of benefits would result. Firstly, he would gain the support of the Conservatives and the Centre Parties and thus reduce his dependence on the Liberals. Secondly, there would also be a financial advantage. Under the 1871 constitution, the federal government depended on customs and excise duties for its revenue. Increased tariffs would guarantee valuable fixed income and bring financial stability for the federal government.

In the *Reichstag* elections of 1877 the National Liberals lost heavily and Bismarck saw the opportunity to dump his Liberal allies. However, for Bismarck to create a new political alliance with the Conservatives and the Centre Party the *Kulturkampf* would have to be resolved.

On the international front, the *Kulturkampf* was also causing Bismarck difficulties. In 1875, a new government was elected in France which was sympathetic to the Centre Party. To Bismarck it now appeared that his struggle was forging an international alliance against Germany, one of the outcomes he had sought to prevent when launching the campaign. Further, he was moving towards the idea of an alliance with Catholic Austria–Hungary and the *Kulturkampf* was proving a stumbling block to this. Finally, he now regarded the socialists within Germany, with their calls for international brotherhood and worldwide revolution, as a greater threat to the empire than the Catholics, who were also anti-socialist in outlook. The *Kulturkampf* had served its purpose but it was now time to reconsider.

The ending of *Kulturkampf*

The death of Pius IX in 1878, and the election of Leo XIII, who was more suited to seek a reconciliation, helped Bismarck's cause. This encouraged the Centre Party to support the German Reich. From then on, its sole concern was with the position of the Catholics in Germany, no matter what government was in power. At home the fall in support for the National Liberals from 127 to 98 seats in the 1878 *Reichstag* elections also confirmed Bismarck's view that his alliance with them had outlived its usefulness. He had now become convinced of the need for tariff reform and worked to build a pro-protectionist alliance in the *Reichstag*, a policy in complete opposition to Liberal ideology.

The change in policy began with a stinging attack on Falk by Bismarck, blaming the former for the excesses of the *Kulturkampf*. Falk resigned and this was followed by the repeal of many, but not all, of the May Laws, and

by 1885, the position of Germany's Catholic minority was more secure within the Reich. On the other hand, the Centre Party did realise that it would be wise to work with rather than against the might of the new German state. There is little doubt that Bismarck had underestimated his opponent, and indeed that the *Kulturkampf* was actually creating more disunity within the Reich. In truth, the campaign had been neither effective nor necessary. On the other hand, never again would the Centre Party threaten Bismarck's position and it had now accepted the right of the Reich to exist. In this political context, it must be concluded that Bismarck had won a partial victory.

Either way, by 1879, the *Kulturkampf* was ended and Bismarck's co-operation with the Liberals was over.

The next enemy

The socialists were an obvious next target for Bismarck. He was concerned about the growth in socialist support since they were anti-monarchist and took an international outlook before their national loyalties.

In 1871, the socialists had won two seats in the *Reichstag*, growing to 9 in the 1874 election and had achieved 12 seats by 1877. In 1875 the Social Democratic Party was formed and its 'Gotha Programme' called for the nationalisation of the banks, coal mines and factories and for social equality. Thus, Bismarck viewed them as a threat to society and they, too, were labelled *Reichsfeinden*.

It is fair to say that Bismarck misjudged his enemy. Only this time, instead of underestimating their strength, he overestimated it. Although the language of the socialists was revolutionary, in practice the leaders were more interested in improving the day-to-day working and living conditions of their members by working within the established political system.

Bismarck never understood the needs of the emerging working classes in Germany and his first response was to try to crush the SPD. But Bismarck's first move against the socialists was a failure. In 1876, he proposed a Bill to prohibit the publication of socialist propaganda. His Liberal allies at the time thought it went too far in trying to control the press and rejected the Bill. However, in 1878 events moved in Bismarck's favour. On 11 May 1878, there was an attempt on the life of the emperor by a socialist and Bismarck immediately proposed an Anti-Socialist Bill. There was little evidence to support his claim that the assassination bid was backed by the socialists and the *Reichstag* rejected the Bill. However, on 2 June, a second, more serious, assassination bid gave Bismarck the excuse he needed. The emperor was persuaded to dissolve the *Reichstag* and new elections were held amidst Bismarck's furious attacks upon the socialists. He also accused

any political party which stood in the way of his proposed new Bill of being unpatriotic. The result of the election was as Bismarck had hoped. The Liberals lost 40 seats, with the Conservatives gaining 37. With reluctance, the new Anti-Socialist Bill was passed by the *Reichstag* in October 1878.

Its terms were harsh:

- all socialist clubs and meetings were banned
- socialist publications were forbidden
- socialists stirring up protests could be exiled
- police powers were increased.

Due to the terms of the *Sozialistgesetz* (Anti-Socialist Act), Bismarck had to agree to a compromise of its being valid for only 30 months in order to have the Bill accepted. However, the Act was renewed repeatedly until the fall of Bismarck from power in 1890.

The effect of the legislation was that many socialists were imprisoned or removed from their homes and sent to remote parts of the Reich. Despite this, like the Catholic Party, the socialists flourished under persecution, their vote increasing between 1878 and 1887 to 750,000.

Source 7.5

'The arrow is aimed at the Social Democrats; but what if it flies over the target?' Cartoon about the reading of the *Sozialistgesetz* (anti-Socialist law) in the Reichstag, 1878.

Aware of this setback, Bismarck now changed tack. He decided to encourage the workers of Germany into supporting the new empire by establishing the world's first state welfare system. However, this too, was to be unsuccessful in that the workers were well aware that the stick of the law had been replaced by the carrot of social welfare. He had hoped that the workers would be grateful to the new regime for this welfare provision but they saw it for what is was – a bribe! They regarded the reforms as no more than 'crumbs from the rich man's table'.

> The scale of his social legislation was at this time unique and enough to establish his reputation as a constructive statesman even if he had done nothing else.
>
> DG Williamson, Bismarck and Germany, 1986.

What reforms did Bismarck enact?

- 1883 – **Sickness Insurance Act** provided medical treatment and up to 13 weeks' sick pay to 3 million low paid workers and their families. This was funded through a contributory system where the workers paid in two thirds and the employer one third.
- 1884 – **Accident Insurance Act** provided cover if a worker was permanently disabled or sick for more than 13 weeks.
- 1886 – **The Accident Insurance Act** was extended to cover 7 million farm workers.
- 1889 – **Old Age and Disability Act** provided pensions for the over 70s and a disability pension to those who were younger.

Although a world first, the welfare legislation was a political failure as the workers well understood that it had been passed out of fear of socialism. Bismarck had hoped it would make the German people 'more contented and easier to manage.' In reality it increased resentment at the obvious political juggling of 'whips and sugar plums' as his policy was called at the time.

Germany and the international community

Germany was a newcomer to the international stage. It was regarded with suspicion by all the other powers as it had fought three wars in nine years to achieve unification. No one believed Bismarck when he claimed that Germany had no more territorial ambitions in Europe.

Given this situation, Bismarck believed that Germany would have to try to prevent wars between the other Great Powers and avoid having to choose between Austria–Hungary and Russia since any choice would leave France free to ally with the unsuccessful power. As McKichan wrote, 'Convinced that his government had little to gain and much to lose in a new armed struggle, he [Bismarck] laboured unceasingly to maintain harmony among the Great Powers.'

The problem was that it would become increasingly difficult 'to maintain harmony among the Great Powers' for a variety of reasons and there was no shortage of world hotspots.

Firstly, in the Near East, there was the Turkish Empire which had been accurately described as 'the sick man of Europe' by the Emperor of Russia. The problem was that as Turkish power declined there was competition between Austria–Hungary and Russia to dominate the Balkan region and this was a source of potential conflict. Bismarck needed to keep on good terms with both and try to stop them fighting each other.

In Africa, 90% of that continent was already divided up among the Great Powers in the 'Scramble for Africa' and thus there was plenty of opportunity for tension.

In the Far East, there was naval competition for strategic bases and also for the establishment of trading posts from which to launch economic penetration of the Pacific countries.

Finally, in Europe, France was set on revenge against Germany, Britain was suspicious of Germany while a possible ally, Austria–Hungary, was too weak to be of much use.

It is no exaggeration to say that between 1871 and 1890, Berlin became the focus for international negotiating, intrigue and treaty making under the direction of Bismarck.

The *Dreikaiserbund* (League of the Three Emperors) was one of Bismarck's first actions to stabilise Europe and win friends and began in 1873. The Tsar of Russia and the Emperors of both Austria–Hungary and Germany agreed to consult on matters of common concern and to agree a collective line of policy. This was an attempt to keep Austria–Hungary and Russia in the same camp. Bismarck had used the fear of Republican France to drive the three leaders together. However, the difficulty of maintaining this was shown in 1875 when, fearful of a revitalised France under the leadership of General McMahon, Bismarck used French army reforms to sabre rattle. He had a series of articles published in the German press under the title, 'Is war in sight?'. To the rest of Europe, it appeared that Bismarck was about to launch a pre-emptive strike against France. Britain, and more significantly Russia, warned Germany that they would not allow France to be attacked again. Bismarck had to retreat from the crisis he himself had created. This showed that he could not depend entirely on the friendship of Russia.

Bismarck's Reich

The Balkans was to provide the stage for the next crisis. In July 1875, Turkish power in the Balkans collapsed. Both Russia and Austria–Hungary were keen to exploit this for selfish ends. After much talking and much slaughter by the Turks and their subject peoples, Russia finally declared war on Turkey in 1877. Turkey was in no position to resist and Russia enforced a tough treaty on Turkey at San Stefano in 1878. This upset the other European powers, especially Britain and Austria–Hungary, who refused to accept the outcome of the war which had greatly increased the influence of Russia in the Balkans. They demanded revision of the treaty. Here was the scenario Bismarck feared. Austria–Hungary and Russia at loggerheads with one another and he having to choose between them. To avoid this, he proposed a conference be held in Berlin to resolve the dispute. He cast himself in the role of 'honest broker' as he argued that Germany was not part of the dispute and had no private interest in the outcome. However, the Congress of Berlin was already a done deal before the representatives of the Great Powers met. Britain and Austria–Hungary had already agreed that Russian gains had to be reduced and there was little Bismarck could do to overturn this.

The Tsar of Russia was furious at Bismarck for his refusal to back the Russian position, commenting that at Berlin there had been, 'a European conspiracy against Russia under the leadership of Prince Bismarck.'

To make matters worse a delighted Austria–Hungary gave Germany permission to retain Schleswig without holding the plebiscite agreed under the 1866 peace treaty. To Russia, it appeared as if Germany was receiving its reward for the position at Berlin. Thus, Bismarck had failed to maintain good relations with both Austria–Hungary and Russia.

This failure and Russia's anti-Bismarck attitude both help to explain Bismarck's next move. In 1879, he signed the secret Dual Alliance with Austria–Hungary. This tied Germany and its southern neighbour together. However, as Austria–Hungary would not guarantee support for Germany if it was at war with France the Alliance did not provide Bismarck with the security he sought for the Reich. At home the Alliance was popular with the southern German states, the National Liberals, the Conservatives and the army. But it was anti-Russian in essence, Germany and Austria–Hungary guaranteeing that, if attacked by Russia, they would help each other.

Undaunted, Bismarck still sought Russian friendship. When the Tsar suggested a renewal of the 1873 League, Bismarck welcomed the opportunity. The three emperors now agreed that if one member were attacked by a fourth power, the other two would remain neutral. Additionally, the Balkans was divided into 'spheres of influence' with Austria–Hungary being dominant in the west and Russia in the east. As DG Williamson noted, however, 'The *Dreikaiserbündnis* was little more

than an armistice as it did not remove the long-term causes of Austro-Russian rivalry in the Balkans.'

Despite this agreement, Bismarck now sought to enlarge the Dual Alliance with Austria–Hungary. Trying to divert French attention from Alsace and Lorraine, the German chancellor encouraged the French to take Tunis in North Africa, knowing full well that Italy, too, wanted this area. Following the French seizure, Bismarck offered Italy the opportunity to join with Germany and Austria–Hungary. Annoyed with France, Italy accepted and thus was formed the Triple Alliance of 1882, guaranteeing that if any signatory power were attacked by France, the others would offer support. If the attack came from another power, the others would remain neutral.

This still did not satisfy Bismarck's desire to protect Germany. In 1883, Austria–Hungary, Germany and Romania signed an alliance, promising to help each other if attacked.

However, the strains on Bismarck's system were beginning to show. In 1887, Russia decided not to renew the *Dreikaiserbündnis* due to its opposition to Austrian ambitions in the Balkans. Anxious to retain Russia's friendship, Bismarck revealed the existence of the Dual Alliance of 1879 without informing Austria–Hungary. There then followed the Re-Insurance Treaty of 1887 between Russia and Germany which promised

Source 7.6

Triple alliance signed on 20 May 1882. Bismarck, Emperor Franz Joseph and King Umberto smoke sitting on a powderkeg.

neutrality from one member if the other was at war, except if Russia attacked Austria–Hungary or Germany attacked France. In return Germany recognised Russian claims in the Balkans.

By the late 1880s, Bismarck was trying to maintain an impossible balance in his diplomacy and his system was under severe strain by the time he fell from power in 1890.

Historians continue to debate Bismarck's foreign policy. AJP Taylor argued in *Bismarck*, that his only object was to maintain the peace of Europe. On the other hand, William Carr argued that, while he did not want war, Bismarck was aided in his quest to keep the peace by the fact that the other European nations also shared this ambition. As to its legacy, Gordon Craig noted in *Germany 1866–1945*, that the Bismarckian system was a very complicated one and its 'complications were the germs of future trouble'. What is certain is that it was in the area of foreign policy that he came into conflict with Emperor William II and this contributed to his resignation in 1890.

Germany's colonial ambitions

To add to this complicated diplomatic situation, there is also the need to address the issue of Germany's imperial policy. In 1880, Bismarck famously stated that he had no interest in acquiring colonies. Such a policy, he knew, would require a navy for their defence and that this would bring Germany into conflict with Britain. Nor does it appear that he was ever won over by the economic argument that colonies would provide new markets for German goods and raw materials for the mother country.

Yet between 1884 and 1885 in particular, Bismarck acquired a colonial empire for Germany. Why the change of heart?

He was under pressure from German missionaries and traders to acquire the areas in which they were active. More importantly, in 1882 the *Kolonialverband* (Colonial League) was set up with the aim of Germany acquiring colonies to establish its place as a Great Power. As Williamson commented, 'There was an element of opportunism in Bismarck's colonial policy,' in that it was the domestic situation which influenced his change of mind. By the mid 1880s, it was obvious that Emperor William I would not live much longer. The Crown Prince, Frederick, married to the daughter of Queen Victoria, was in favour of a reform of the German constitution to make it more democratic and akin to that of Britain. Bismarck opposed such moves and in order to reduce the influence of the Crown Prince, it is argued that he tried to place the latter in a no-win situation. Frederick was supported in his policy of constitutional reform by the National Liberals in the *Reichstag*. They opposed the idea of German imperial expansion. By acquiring an empire, Bismarck hoped to

isolate the Crown Prince. He could hardly disagree with the idea of German expansion as he would appear unpatriotic and his support would destroy his Liberal alliance.

In the event, Bismarck need not have worried, for Frederick would reign for less than 100 days. With the hands of the Crown Prince now seemingly firmly tied, Bismarck rapidly lost interest in the colonial issue. Colonies proved to be a burden both financially and administratively and did little to help the growth of the German economy. As with so many other aspects of the career of Bismarck, it was the colonial legacy that would haunt Germany. The desertion of the colonial issue by 1889 brought him into conflict with Emperor William II and would contribute to his downfall. In the longer term, his imperial policy would bring Germany into conflict with Britain, and that would have serious consequences.

Activity ⮕

Imagine that you are a researcher working for Otto von Bismarck just after his resignation in 1890. You have been asked to prepare a report favourable to Bismarck's memory, outlining his work after unification and explaining why it was so important for Germany. However, you are aware that there are other researchers keen to discredit Bismarck.

In your report:

- Describe briefly the work of Bismarck as Chancellor of Germany.

- Provide evidence to support your argument that Bismarck's work was hugely important and beneficial to Germany. Identify and comment on any arguments that may be presented by those who oppose your views.

In your report you must use extensive detailed knowledge.

Present your report in written form or as an oral presentation lasting between 4 and 6 minutes.

Exam essays 📄

Ultimately Bismarck's policies as Chancellor between 1871 and 1890 were failures. Do you agree, with reference to either his domestic or foreign policies?

Dropping the Pilot: the *Kaiserreich*

Introduction

Bismarck's dominance in Germany ended in 1890. His position weakened in 1888 when the new 29-year-old William II became emperor. The new emperor and his chancellor had different views over which direction Germany should now take.

Domestically, William II wanted a united people behind him as he prepared for a world role for Germany. He was sympathetic to groups like the *Kolonialverband*. Additionally, the emperor saw little point in trying to maintain Russian friendship and wanted a closer working relationship with Austria–Hungary.

Other forces were working for the removal of Bismarck. Ambitious politicians were frustrated by their inability to rise to the highest office in the land due to Bismarck monopolising the chancellorship. Even worse, he appeared to be grooming his son, Herbert, to succeed him. Even the army now wanted to see him go.

Bismarck's downfall

Two crises led to the downfall of 'the pilot' who had guided the German ship of state since its inception. At home, the anti-socialist law was due for renewal. Bismarck wanted it strengthened, believing that only force could smash the socialists. He proposed a new, much stricter law, adding that it should become permanent. When it became obvious that the *Reichstag* would not pass this measure, he then persuaded the Conservative deputies to vote against renewal of the existing legislation. He apparently believed that once socialist activity was legal, they would rise up in revolt and the army would then crush the menace once and for all. This failed to materialise.

Diplomatically, the emperor refused to sanction the renewal of the Re-Insurance Treaty with Russia. News of Russian troop movements near Germany's eastern border caused him to demand German mobilisation. Bismarck realised this would merely inflame the situation and persuaded the emperor to step back from the brink. Bismarck then accused William II of interfering with foreign policy. This was too much for the headstrong young ruler. In the row which followed, Bismarck offered to resign – an offer promptly accepted. Bismarck believed that popular opposition to his removal would see him back in office but a new generation of Germans had grown up with no particular loyalty to him and Bismarck was now an old man.

> By 1890, Bismarck appeared to have exhausted his genius for improvisation and to have had no other answer for the problems of his society but violence.
>
> DG Williamson, Bismarck and Germany, 1986.

Source 8.1

'Dropping the Pilot', *Punch*, March 20, 1890

Bismarck spent his eight years in retirement writing his memoirs in which he set out to justify his actions during his political career. As always, he was to have the last word. His tombstone bore the inscription, 'Bismarck, Loyal and True Servant of William I'.

The great man had gone. What type of new Germany would now emerge?

Germany under Emperor William II

There is little doubt that Bismarck's departure was popular amongst many sections of German society. The new, young Germany looked forward to a bright future under the leadership of the twenty-nine-year-old Emperor William II. But there is little doubt that he was not best suited for the personal rule that he wanted to establish after 1890. He tired quickly of government papers and business, was absent from Berlin a lot and often rushed into decisions before weighing up all of the evidence. He would often also contradict himself, supporting one group at any given time, and then switching his support to their rivals. This is shown by his support of the working-class in 1890, followed by his demands for repression in 1905. Similarly, in 1892 he was opposed to tariffs but supported them in 1904. He had no consistent domestic policies.

Dropping the Pilot: the *Kaiserreich*

> *Above all, William was determined to establish what he thought would be personal rule. Instead he was the one constant, unavoidable, unpredictable factor with which all statesmen had to reckon.*
>
> Ian Porter and Ian Armour, Imperial Germany, 1991.

On the domestic front, Germany continued to make rapid industrial progress. This was fuelled by the exploitation of the mineral-rich areas of Alsace and Lorraine, taken from France in 1871. In addition, Germany was a world leader in the chemical and electrical industries. Companies such as IG Farben and Siemens were pioneering new applications for their industries. Rudolf Diesel developed the heavy oil engine which bears his name. All of these developments meant that Germany was gaining ground on British industrial supremacy and the constant demand for new materials and new markets was an important issue in Germany's drive to acquire a colonial empire. However, not all areas were making such progress. The farming sector in particular was vulnerable to foreign, especially American and Russian, imports and this led successive German chancellors to support protectionism and align with the Conservative Party.

Nonetheless, the governments under William II did pass some important legislation to help the under-privileged groups in German society. In 1891, Sunday working was abolished and a guaranteed minimum wage was introduced. In 1901, industrial arbitration courts became compulsory, and this was followed by an extension of health insurance and additional controls on child labour in 1903. In 1911, insurance was extended to all salaried employees. Thus, in terms of social welfare, Germany had established a scheme which was the envy of the world.

There were also some changes in the political scene as well. In 1904, the Polling Booth Law improved provision for secret ballots at election time, and in 1906 payment for *Reichstag* deputies was introduced, However, the *Junkers* and their supporters continued to dominate the largest state in Germany, despite their numerical inferiority. Another aspect of the regime that tarnished its reputation abroad was the poor treatment of Germany's ethnic minorities, particularly the Poles and the Jews.

Politically, the period was marked by the continuing increased support for the socialist SPD. The Bismarckian anti-social laws were not renewed and with the new freedoms the party now enjoyed, it thrived. This support from the working classes was a great disappointment to the emperor who believed that this group owed him a debt of loyalty for removing the hostile legislation. The growth in support for the SPD reached its peak in the *Reichstag* elections of 1912, when it won 33% of the popular vote and it became the largest single party in the *Reichstag*. Like Bismarck, the

emperor did not seem to have a coherent policy to meet the needs of his working-class citizens and he, too, was defeated by forces he did not fully understand. What the emperor and his supporters failed to perceive was that the SPD was more interested in improvements to working and living conditions than the creation of a revolution. This led to a split between the workers demanding greater rights and the landowners and factory owners who refused to give up any of their power and wealth. Again, Porter and Armour commented, 'German society was divided in terms of class'.

Changes to German foreign policy

From 1890, there was a notable change in German foreign policy. The emperor was determined that Germany should play a world role in international diplomacy, and to some extent he was influenced by groups such as the Pan-German League (*Alldeutscher Verband*) and the *Kolonialverband*, as well as by the Prussian Chiefs of Staff and his naval secretary, von Tirpitz.

The caution of Bismarck was swept aside, as shown by the decision not to renew the Reinsurance Treaty with Russia which now turned increasingly towards France for support. There was also the belief, noted by McKichan, that, 'Germany was too powerful to need the kind of under-hand double dealing implicit in this [Reinsurance] treaty.'

The other notable feature of this new German diplomacy was the gradual cooling of relations with Britain and its move, slowly but perceptibly, towards a greater friendship with France and Russia. Before 1890, Britain and Germany had enjoyed relatively good diplomatic relations but when the emperor praised the South African Boer president, Paul Kruger, for his stance against Britain, the British public became suspicious of, and indeed hostile towards, Germany.

The emperor was also determined to establish what was referred to as *Weltpolitik*. Porter and Armour describe this as, 'a coherent drive for world power,' and is illustrated by William II's drive to establish a German navy to help Germany establish 'her place in the sun'. The construction and widening of the Kiel Canal, which would give German battleships rapid access to the North Sea, and the Naval Laws of 1898 and 1900 were all viewed by Britain as a threat to its naval supremacy.

Britain's response was to modernise the Royal Navy from 1904 onwards, and to begin construction of the *Dreadnought-class* battleship fleet, prompting Germany to respond with its *Nassau-class* ships. Naval rivalry certainly soured relations between the two powers. Despite efforts on the part of the emperor to reach a *rapprochement* (an attempt to re-establish friendly relations with another country) with Britain, the two powers continued to drift apart in the years prior to the outbreak of war in 1914.

Dropping the Pilot: the *Kaiserreich*

For Germany, France was always a potential enemy. When the 1904 Entente Cordiale between Britain and France was signed, Germany feared it was an anti-German move. Thus, it could be argued that Germany's clumsy intervention in the Moroccan Crisis of 1905 was designed to split this new understanding between two old rivals. At the conference to decide what should happen, Germany found itself isolated, with only the support of its ally Austria–Hungary. This reinforced German reliance upon its southern neighbour. German fear of encirclement was heightened by the signing of the Anglo-Russian Entente in 1907. This Triple Entente provoked a hysterical reaction within Germany, with the chancellor, von Bülow, angrily commenting that:

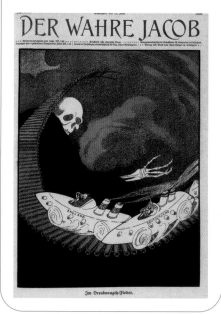

Source 8.2

In Dreadnought-Fever – Caricature on the arms race in building heavy battleships between Germany and Great Britain.

DER WAHRE JACOB

Im Dreadnought-Fieber.

> "
> A policy aimed at the encirclement of Germany and seeking to form a ring of powers in order to isolate and paralyse it would be disastrous to the peace of Europe. The formation of such a ring around Germany would not be possible without exerting some pressure. Pressure gives rise to counter-pressure. And out of this pressure and counter-pressure finally explosions may arise.
>
> *Prince von Bülow, 1907.*

A second German attempt to split the Entente Powers occurred in 1911, when the emperor visited the port of Agadir in Morocco, demanding that all powers should have equal access to Morocco, then under French control. Once more this backfired, as Britain feared Germany was trying to establish a naval base in North Africa, an area that was regarded as vital to the Royal Navy. In 1912, the Anglo–French Naval Accord made provision for British defence of the French Channel coast and its western coastline, while France agreed to protect British interests in the Mediterranean. As a result, the German fleet operating in the North Sea would have to face the bulk of the Royal Navy in time of war. There is little doubt that both of these German interventions in Morocco helped to strengthen Anglo–French relations.

Source 8.3

Map of German colonies in Africa.

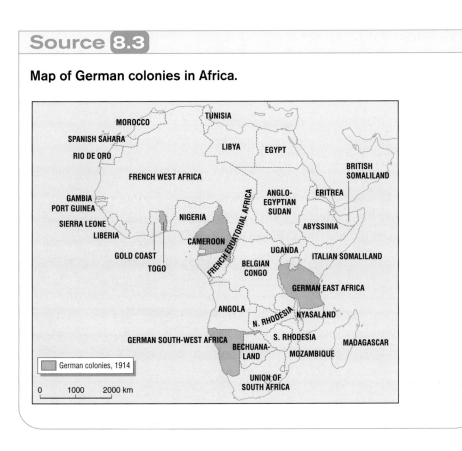

MOROCCO
TUNISIA
SPANISH SAHARA
LIBYA
EGYPT
RIO DE ORO
BRITISH
SOMALILAND
FRENCH WEST AFRICA
ANGLO-
EGYPTIAN
SUDAN
ERITREA
GAMBIA
PORT GUINEA
NIGERIA
ABYSSINIA
SIERRA LEONE
LIBERIA
CAMEROON
FRENCH EQUATORIAL AFRICA
UGANDA
ITALIAN SOMALILAND
GOLD COAST
BELGIAN
CONGO
TOGO
GERMAN EAST AFRICA
ANGOLA
NYASALAND
N. RHODESIA
GERMAN SOUTH-WEST AFRICA
S. RHODESIA
MADAGASCAR
BECHUANA-
LAND
MOZAMBIQUE
German colonies, 1914
UNION OF
SOUTH AFRICA
0   1000   2000 km

Germany and World War One

Bismarck had once noted that the Balkans was 'not worth the bones of a
Pomeranian grenadier', yet it was to be in this area that World War One
was to erupt. German economic penetration of the area had already begun,
with its financing of the Berlin to Baghdad railway in the late nineteenth
century. In 1912, the First Balkan War broke out, when the last remnants
of Turkish power in Europe were destroyed by the alliance of Serbia,
Greece and Bulgaria. However, the Great Powers were concerned at the
growth in strength of these Balkan countries and demanded that the final
decision be made by an international conference in London. The 1913
Treaty of London had upset the pre-war agreements between the Balkan
League members. In particular, in order to stop the growth of Serbia,
Austria–Hungary demanded the creation of a new state of Albania to cut-
off Serbia from access to the sea. As a result of these changes, the members
of the Balkan League fell out with one another. War was renewed in the
Second Balkan War, the victor being Serbia which nearly doubled in size,
increasing Austrian anxiety about the threat of Slav nationalism to the
existence of its multi-ethnic empire. Austria–Hungary then looked for an
excuse to crush Serbia. That came with the assassination of the Archduke
Franz Ferdinand on 28 June 1914.

Article 231 of the Treaty of Versailles essentially blamed Germany for the outbreak of the war. Was this the case? Fritz Fischer has controversially argued so:

> " The German Government was determined from early July 1914 to use this favourable opportunity for a war against France and Russia.
>
> Fritz Fischer, War of Illusions, 1969.

Certainly, the German decision to give wholehearted support to Austria–Hungary in its dealings with Serbia was an important factor in Vienna's decision to issue its ultimatum in July 1914. That ultimatum, described by Sir Edward Grey, British Foreign Secretary, as, 'The most formidable document that I have ever seen addressed by one state to another that is independent,' led to a series of attempts to defuse the crisis. Austria–Hungary was encouraged by Berlin to reject all of these. With the ultimatum being delivered, there can be little doubt that Austria–Hungary believed it had the long awaited opportunity to deal with Serbia once and for all. Russia was now called upon to defend its ally Serbia, which it did in a half-hearted and faltering way, not agreeing to full mobilisation until 31 July. The German response was to declare war on Russia.

Now Germany was trapped by what AJP Taylor described as 'war by timetable' because once the Schlieffen Plan was launched, there was no way to reverse or cancel it. German declaration of war on France and the invasion of Belgium prompting British support under the 1839 Treaty of London transformed the quarrel between Austria–Hungary and Serbia into a global conflict. As Finlay McKichan summed it up, 'German nationalism and determination to be recognised as a world power played a large part in bringing about World War One.'

By the end of the war the empire which Bismarck had created and determined to protect would be destroyed and one of his *Reichsfeinden*, the socialists, would inherit the system he had created to protect Prussia and its monarchy.

Source 8.4

'German is your language and pure German is your method of advertising.'

Activity ▐▐▶

In this activity devise at least 10 key questions that would test someone's understanding of the main issues and developments associated with the Kaiser's Germany between 1980 and 1914. This requires careful consideration but will enhance your understanding of the topic.

To construct questions, first understand the issues that you are assessing and ensure your questions are not vague or ambiguous, but focus attention on the key issue. Questions should be relevant and well presented and should test real understanding. They should be open-ended and avoid one-word responses. The purpose is to aid learning, not to confuse by asking obscure or tricky questions.

When your list is complete, try them out on a partner. Can he or she answer your questions? Can you answer your partner's questions?

Questions that were wrongly answered or did not have a response should be the focus for future study.

Exam essays 🗐

To what extent do you accept the view that between 1890 and 1914 the Kaiser's Germany became undemocratic and internationally aggressive?

Dropping the Pilot: the *Kaiserreich*

The Weimar Republic

Events in Germany, 1918–1920

Source 9.1

28 September 1918
Surrender of Bulgaria.

October 1918
General Staff insist upon democratisation of the German government.
Prince Max von Baden becomes chancellor, responsible to the Reichstag.

29 October 1918
Mutiny begins in the German navy at Kiel.

30 October 1918
Surrender of Turkey.

November 3 1918
Surrender of Austria–Hungary.

4 November 1918
Kiel mutinies spread.

November 9 1918
General strike in Berlin.
Abdication of the emperor announced.
Ebert, leader of the socialist SPD became chancellor.
Germany asks Allies for an armistice.

November 11 1918
Armistice comes into effect.

January 1919
Attempted coup by extreme left-wing – the Spartacist Uprising. This is crushed by the army and the Freikorps.
SPD wins the largest number of seats in the *Reichstag*, but falls short of an overall majority. Coalition government formed.

June 28 1919
Treaty of Versailles signed. Bitter opposition to the terms of this treaty within Germany.

January 1920
Attempted right-wing coup – the Kapp *Putsch*. The German army was sympathetic to the coup which was suppressed by the calling of a general strike amongst German workers.

As the timeline indicates, the new country had to face several severe challenges to its very existence in its formative years. Simpson believes that:

> *The Weimar Republic was born out of the external defeat of the German Empire and the internal collapse of its system of government. It is an open question whether the Weimar Republic could ever have overcome the disadvantages which attended its birth.*

Certainly large sections of the population and the media were hostile to the new Republic from the very beginning and Finlay McKichan has put forward the theory that this was, 'a Republic nobody wanted'. He supports this by the argument that:

- democratic reforms were only introduced in October 1918 in a deliberate attempt to gain better terms from the Allies
- the revolution of November 1918 was not extensive enough
- there were divisions among those who claimed to be the supporters of the regime.

What evidence is there to support this view?

It is argued that military defeat was not accompanied by real political change. During the war the German Empire had effectively been run by Generals Hindenburg and Ludendorff. Following the breakthrough of the German trenches by the Allies in August 1918, it was these leaders who argued for a 'revolution from above', controlling the revolution and avoiding the chaos of Russia in the immediate aftermath of the November Revolution of 1917. This led to the appointment of Prince Max von Baden, with the view that such a liberal civilian government would achieve better terms with the Allies at any future peace conference. This 'revolution from above' resulted in a number of changes to the way Germany was run.

The army now came under the control of the civilian government, rather than the emperor. For the first time, ministers were now responsible to the *Reichstag* and the formerly undemocratic voting system in Prussia was reformed to give 'one man, one vote'. The negative side of such positive developments was that the new leaders of Germany were the ones who had to carry the burden of Germany's defeat and not the emperor and his generals, who were now regarded as national heroes in the nostalgic eyes of many people.

However, there were developments elsewhere that threatened this peaceful transition of power. As in Russia, workers' and soldiers' soviets had appeared. These groups, or 'councils', demanded a much more thorough

Source 9.2

Rally, which ended in fighting in front of the Reichstag against the Works Councils Law. This was a demonstration against the Works Council Law.

change in the way Germany was ruled and mutinies broke out in the German navy. These spread rapidly and law and order appeared to be under threat. This forced the new government to make an alliance with the army in order to restore order, which was to have long-lasting implications for the new regime.

Supporters of the revolution were also divided, as John Hiden notes.

> *Although the time seemed ripe for a remodelling of society and a clean break with the imperial past, German socialists were neither fully prepared for revolution nor united.*
>
> John Hiden, *The Weimar Republic*, 1974.

The socialists, under Ebert who now led the government, had been brought up in the tradition of moving towards an improvement in working and living conditions by working within the established political system They were unlikely to provide the dynamic leadership which could exploit the new situation. Indeed, the socialists themselves were divided. The extreme left-wing of the party had already split, forming the Independent Socialists, or USPD, which opposed the war and refused to cooperate with the emperor's government. They also refused to work with Ebert.

Thus, the opportunities presented by the abdication of the emperor could not be fully exploited to the benefit of the new regime. Evidence to support the idea of a 'missed opportunity' include:

- The secret agreements made between the leaders of the new government and the Army, the latter only giving its consent when it became clear that the new leadership would not pursue any revolutionary ideas and that there would be respect for law and order. John Hiden has argued that, 'the SPD leadership remained committed to suppressing threats from extremists, which was wholly consistent with Ebert's own conception of the revolution as the moderate democratisation of the German state.'

- The agreement reached between the employers and the major industrial firms. This resulted in the German revolution taking a quite different path from that of Russia. Instead of workers overthrowing employers, in Germany, they continued to co-operate in order to preserve the peace. Such a tactic had the added benefit of avoiding any marked deterioration in workers' living standards by maintaining full employment. This agreement was bitterly opposed by the workers' and soldiers' councils.

What was Ebert to do? In justification of his policy, he argued that he had no choice.

> *We had to make sure that the Reich machine did not break down; that it was able to maintain our food supplies and the economy. The six of us [the leaders of the government] could not do that alone; we needed the experienced co-operation of experts. We would have faced failure in a few days. We therefore urgently appealed to all Reich officials to continue to exercise their duty until further notice.*
>
> — *Friedrich Ebert.*

Historians, too, have tried to defend the actions of Ebert.

> *Ebert and his Social Democrat colleagues were eager to re-establish order in Germany and to organise the election of a National Assembly. They had no reason to believe that the sort of Germany they wanted could not be created without the aid of existing officials.*
>
> *AJ Nicholls, Weimar and the Rise of Hitler, 1970.*

Finlay McKichan adds that, 'The Social Democrats seemed less concerned to keep on good terms with the Independent Socialists who were members of the same government', implying that the creation of stable government

The Weimar Republic

Germany 1815–1939

was more important than any idea of working-class solidarity. AJ Ryder, in *The German Revolution*, sums up the events of 1918 as the need to:

1. Democratise the government.
2. Demilitarise the apparatus of the state by creating a people's army.
3. Achieve the more even spread of wealth throughout society.

Ebert and his supporters felt this could be best achieved within the existing political structures.

Meanwhile several main issues threatened the security of the new Republic – pressure from left- and right-wing political parties, the impact of the treaty of Versailles, the Constitution and economic instability.

Internal enemies

In January 1919, the leaders of the USPD, Karl Liebknecht and Rosa Luxemburg, supported an armed uprising, known to history as the 'Spartacist Rebellion'.

It was now that the alliance of the new government and the old imperial army came into operation. Ebert feared for the existence of his government and he urged the army to suppress the rebellion, believing that the gains from November 1918 would be lost. Employing returning ex-soldiers in groups known as *Freikorps*, the state used all means at its disposal to suppress the uprising. No mercy was shown, with Liebknecht and Luxemburg being murdered before they could stand trial. This action destroyed any hope of co-operation between the different wings of the socialist groups, with the USPD refusing ever again to work with the majority socialists, even when faced by the dangers posed by Hitler and his party.

The Treaty of Versailles

Another major factor was the fact that the new Weimar Government had to deal with the consequences of the Treaty of Versailles. Here was a classic example of the old regime escaping its responsibility for the defeat of Germany in 1918.

It was up to the new rulers of Germany to accept the terms of the treaty, or risk the renewal of war. Thus the German delegates who stood before the Allied leaders in June 1919 were mere puppets and the only group to emerge untainted by Versailles was the officer corps of the old Imperial German army. Such an escape gave rise to the myth of the 'stab in the back', popularised by Hitler, amongst others. This claimed that the German army had been undefeated in 1918 (like all myths, it did contain an element of truth, as German soldiers still occupied areas of north-eastern France in November 1918), and that it was the discontents at home, the democrats,

the Jews, the communists and the socialists, that had forced Germany into the armistice of November 1918, with all its consequences. The reality was that the German army was about to collapse, and the democratisation of Germany in October 1918 was a ploy on the part of Hindenburg and Ludendorff to squeeze better peace terms from Germany's enemies.

However, there is little doubt that the stigma of the so-called 'November criminals' hung like a giant shadow over the period of Weimar Germany.

The Treaty of Versailles ran to some 440 clauses. Individually, each could be justified, but the cumulative effect of its demands appeared to most Germans as a punishment for losing what they had long believed was a 'defensive war'.

There were several major areas of complaint.

The first was the loss of territory. Although France regained Alsace and Lorraine, most Germans probably expected to lose these provinces as Germany had taken them from France at the end of the war of 1870–71, the people spoke French and their restoration to France had been a mainstay of French foreign policy from that date.

In addition, the Saar coalfields were to be transferred to France for fifteen years as compensation for the German destruction of French coalfields as they retreated in 1918. The final decision as to who would control the area would be made following a plebiscite (a referendum), held in 1935.

On the other hand, land lost to Belgium (Eupen and Malmedy), Denmark (North Schleswig) and to Poland (Posen, West Prussia and the upper part of Silesia) angered many Germans. They believed these changes were contrary to the Allies' own principles, especially US President Woodrow Wilson's desire to see frontiers of the 'new Europe' to be drawn along 'recognisable lines of nationality'. Wilson had also claimed that one of the causes of the war was the existence of many minority peoples living within countries which were alien to their language, culture and tradition. It was difficult to reconcile these ideas with the treaty arrangements which left millions of German-speaking people in the so-called 'Polish Corridor' and that East Prussia was now separated from the rest of the country. Additionally, some three million German-speaking settlers now lived under the government of Czechoslovakia. Similarly, the idea of a union between Austria and Germany (*Anschluss*) was specifically ruled out by the terms of both the Treaties of Versailles and St Germain. On the other hand, allowing such a cultural union of German speakers would have made Germany a larger state than it had been in August 1914, and thus it was unlikely that the Allied powers could ever agree to such terms immediately after four years of bloody conflict.

The Weimar Republic

Internationally, all of Germany's colonies were taken from its control, to be ruled under a mandate from the League of Nations for the benefit of the people living in those areas. In reality, the colonies were given to the victorious powers which had been Germany's imperial rivals in the nineteenth century. Hence, there was a sense of grievance and injustice over these terms.

So although it could be claimed that Wilsonian ideology had been achieved by the creation of new states like Poland and Czechoslovakia, and the creation of the independent countries of Austria and Hungary, the same ideology when applied to the German situation did appear to be somewhat contradictory. In defence of the treaty, however, it should also be mentioned that the fourteen points of Wilson's declaration were not mentioned in the terms of the Armistice of 11 November 1918 and thus the German government should not have claimed later that these were in fact guarantees.

The second cause for complaint was the way the treaty was agreed. In previous conflicts, both sides had sat down to discuss peace terms but on this occasion the Germans were excluded from the preliminary discussions and were handed a draft at the end of May, 1919, which they could accept or reject. Rejection would lead to a renewal of the war. Despite the resignation of the entire German Cabinet, led by Scheidemann, when faced with the treaty terms, the German delegation had no option but to sign the treaty on 28 June 1919. However, the German people and government were never reconciled to the idea of reparations nor German 'war-guilt'.

Hugo Preuss, one of the main architects of the constitution of the Weimar Republic bemoaned the terms of the Treaty for Germany:

> If the empire was born out of the brilliance of victory, the German Republic was born out of its terrible defeat. This difference… cast from the first a dark shadow on the new political order… the criminal madness of the imposed Versailles settlement was a shameless blow… The Reich constitution of Weimar was born with this curse upon it.
>
> — Hugo Preuss.

Another source of dispute was over the disarmament of Germany and there could have been little doubt that a country with such a proud military tradition as Germany would regard the terms as humiliating.

After the losses suffered during the war, the Allies were determined to prevent such a conflict from ever happening again. Even in 1919, the German army consisted of some 300,000 men. By Article 160 of the Treaty, this was to be reduced to 100,000; no conscription was allowed and the officer corps was restricted to less than 4,000 in number.

The German navy was similarly reduced in size, with a ban on possessing any submarines. The German air force was to be abolished. At French insistence, the area on the west bank of the River Rhine and a belt of land to a breadth of 50 kilometres east of the river was to be de-militarised. This was to prevent a future German attack upon France. To ensure that Germany kept to these terms, the Allies set up a control commission. The German military's views of these terms can be seen in the navy's response to the terms. Part of the German fleet had been held at the British naval base at Scapa Flow in the Orkney Islands since 21 November 1918. Rather than risk handing over the fleet to the Allies the Germans scuttled (deliberately sank) their own ships in May 1919.

The Allied claim that Germany had caused the war was also bitterly resented. The reasons for the outbreak of war in 1914 have been the subject of great discussion since 1919. To claim, as did Article 231(the war guilt clause) that Germany and its allies had to accept full responsibility for the war was a gross simplification of the process. From the Allied point of view, Article 231 was inserted to justify the claim for reparation payments from Germany for the losses suffered during the war. In retrospect it is possible to see that demands for compensation, the setting up of a Commission to oversee these payments and French insistence on the timetable being strictly followed were a recipe for future trouble.

Within Germany, the terms of the treaty created an impression of a vindictive Allied plot to humiliate Germany. The treaty was to cast a long shadow over the history of the Weimar Republic, leading some historians to conclude that the treaty was responsible for the support given to the Nazis during the 1920s. AJ Nicholls has written, 'The German public was in no way prepared for a harsh peace… The Imperial government and the emperor were gone, and so the man in the street felt free from all liability for Imperial policies,' and as Hans Kohn has argued they had targets for their blame.

> "
> Many Germans blamed the Allies for the weakness of democratic Germany. The lament of so many decent… Germans about the burdens and cruelties inflicted by the Allies upon an innocent Germany… undermined democracy… and facilitated the rise of Hitler.
>
> Hugo Preuss.

This school of thought argues that the signatories of the treaty, the 'November criminals', had stabbed the German army in the back and betrayed the country by signing a harsh and unjust treaty. Getting rid of the treaty became the central part of the programme of Nationalist and Nazi propaganda.

Perhaps a more balanced view is expressed by John Hiden:

> *The Versailles treaty certainly did not doom the Republic from birth, but it did create particularly troublesome dimensions to existing internal conflicts and contradictions which had, to some extent, survived the revolution.*
>
> John Hiden, The Weimar Republic, 1974.

The long term damage of the treaty is summed up by AJ Nicholls, arguing in *Weimar and the Rise of Hitler* that, 'The real damage the treaty did to Germany was to disillusion more moderate men who might otherwise have supported their new Republic.'

The problems of German democracy

Can a country be too democratic? That is the question that historians have raised since the collapse of the Weimar Republic in January 1933.

The Weimar Constitution has been called 'the world's most perfect democracy – on paper.' For the first time, all Germans, male and female, could vote if over the age of twenty. The *Reichstag* was to be elected directly by the German people while the upper house, the *Reichsrat*, contained representatives of all the German states. Elections were to be determined by a form of proportional representation. This meant that a party obtaining 15% of the total votes cast would receive 15% of the seats in the *Reichstag*.

The president, the head of state, was to be elected directly by the people. He had extensive powers which included:

- being head of the armed forces
- appointing the Reich Chancellor
- having the right to dissolve the *Reichstag* and call fresh elections
- under Article 48, he could suspend the constitution and rule directly by decree in times of crisis.

The difficulties that this constitution produced were, firstly, that proportional representation led to the growth of many small parties.

The number of parties, combined with the proportional representation voting system, made it impossible for any one party to win a majority in the *Reichstag*. Coalition governments (governments made up of two or more political parties) were thus necessary. However, as the political parties had many different ideas as to how the country should be run, these coalitions were difficult to form and even more difficult to maintain. This led to many elections and the appearance of a weak form of government.

The table below shows the major political parties during the 1920s:

Source 9.3

DNVP	German National People's Party
NSDAP	National Socialist German Workers' Party
DVP	German People's Party
Zentrum	Centre Party
DDP	German Democratic Party
SPD	German Socialist Party
USPD	United German Socialist Party
KPD	German Communist Party

Secondly, as head of state, the president could suspend the constitution and rule by himself in times of emergency. On the one hand, it has been argued that this conditioned the German people to the idea of rule by one man and indeed reminded them of the 'Good Old Days' of the Imperial Empire. On the other hand, its use after the collapse of the German economy in October 1929, and the inability of parties to agree terms for a coalition, did help to keep some form of government going during this difficult period.

Although the government had been prepared to use the army and the *Freikorps* to suppress the left-wing uprising of 1919, by the start of 1920 the *Freikorps* in particular were beginning to pose a threat to law and order. In early 1920 the government wanted to disband elements of these units. This led to a march on Berlin by some *Freikorps* members. In terror, the government fled and a new government was declared under Wolfgang Kapp. The German leader, Ebert, asked the army for help. When this was not forthcoming, the government called a general strike. The near paralysis of Berlin as public transport workers, workers in the power industries and even civil servants heeded the call to strike led to the withdrawal of the *Freikorps*.

Evidence of the dependence of the new democratic regime on the power structures of Imperial Germany came to light in the aftermath of this Kapp *Putsch*. Whereas the leaders of the Spartacist uprising had been murdered without trial, the leaders of the 1920 coup were let off fairly lightly.

The lasting impact of this was to destroy any loyalty between the people and government after its escape from Berlin to Weimar.

Economic problems

It is now generally agreed that the idea of war reparations was not very well considered. It was to prove impossible for Germany to meet its treaty obligations of £100 million per year for 66 years. The cost of financing its own war effort and the loss of land and resources under the treaty severely weakened the German economy.

However, the background to the hyper-inflation of 1923 had little to do with economics. In 1922, the German government signed a Treaty of Friendship and co-operation with Russia, the other outcast nation of post-war Europe. Among the secret provisions were clauses allowing German troops to train on Russian territory, thereby avoiding some of the military restrictions of the Treaty of Versailles. News of the treaty was soon common knowledge, and the French in particular were looking for an excuse to put Germany back in its place.

Early in 1923, the Germans had defaulted on payment of telegraph poles and some tons of coal as reparations. Seizing on this, the French and Belgian governments acted jointly to occupy Germany's richest industrial area, the Ruhr. The German government called on the workers of the Ruhr to meet such aggression with passive resistance. In effect, this meant a strike in most industries in the Ruhr. This area was the heart of the German economy. As it slowed, then almost stopped, the effects were soon felt across Germany. Unemployment rocketed and inflation began to run away, as can be seen in the table below.

Source 9.4

Value of US dollar to German Mark	
January 1922	$1=80 Marks
January 1923	$1=18,000 Marks
November 1923	$1=4,420 million Marks

This resulted in the German economy spiralling out of control. People were often paid twice a day; barter replaced cash exchanges, and many middle-class families lost everything that they had saved over generations.

However, the German government can partly be blamed for the impact of hyper-inflation. It certainly suited them since it could now repay debts at a fraction of their real value. It authorised the printing and over-printing of German banknotes without the gold reserves to support it. Those in

Source 9.5

A twenty billion Mark note

circulation lost all face value. People who were in employment were just able to survive, but those on fixed incomes, like pensioners, were ruined. It was this sense of hopelessness and unfairness that led many people yearn for 'the good old days' of strong rule under the emperor. Although the causes of hyper-inflation are extremely complicated, to the ordinary German it was the fault of a government that had accepted reparations payments as part of the Treaty of Versailles and appeared to have played no active part to prevent the crisis of 1923 from deepening. Many, especially amongst the middle-class, never forgave the Weimar Republic for the humiliation that was forced upon them – selling the family possessions, becoming dependent on state or charity hand-outs, etc – and it was this group who were to prove most receptive to the seductive message of Nazism. The economic events of 1923 also led to political consequences, one of which was an attempt by an extreme right-wing group to seize power in Bavaria.

Hoping to capitalise on the misery of 1923, in November Adolf Hitler tried to seize power in Munich and march on Berlin to force the government to give way to a new, right-wing force. However, the event was a fiasco and Hitler was captured, put on trial for treason and sentenced to five years in prison. He was released after less than one year, but the menace of the Nazis had been brought to national attention. Hitler's contempt for Weimar democracy can be seen in this conversation held while prisoner in Landsberg Castle.

Source 9.6

Proclamation of 9 November: Hitler declares the Reich's government deposed.

> *When I begin active work, it will be necessary to pursue a new policy. Instead of working to achieve power by an armed coup, we shall have to hold our noses and enter the Reichstag against the Catholic and Marxist deputies. If outvoting them takes longer than outshooting them, at least the results will be guaranteed by their own Constitution.*
>
> — *Adolf Hitler.*

With the suppression of the Beer Hall *Putsch* (coup) and the arrival of US loans as part of the Dawes Plan, the situation in Weimar Germany began to improve. However, the memory of the 'economic whirlwind' of 1923 was to remain long in the memories of the German people.

A Golden Era?

The time between 1924 and 1929 is often called the 'Golden Era of the Weimar Republic' and coincided with the coming to power of Gustav Stresemann who was German Foreign Minister from 1924 till his death in 1929. Among his achievements, he was able to persuade the French to leave the Ruhr, having promised that Germany would restart payment of reparations. This helped pave the way for the introduction of the new currency in 1924, the *Rentenmark*, which formed part of the Dawes Plan for the economic recovery of Germany. This plan also reduced the burden of German reparation repayments and this was backed by massive foreign loans designed to get German industry back to work. This led to a measure of economic prosperity for Germany. This can be seen in the fact that, although now a smaller country than in 1914, German industrial output in 1927 was higher than at any time since 1913. This recovery from the war compared favourably with the conditions in both Britain and France in the inter-war decade of the 1920s.

In foreign policy, Stresemann was able to end Germany's diplomatic isolation from the rest of Europe. He improved relations with France, agreeing to the Locarno Pact of 1925 which guaranteed the Franco–German border established by the Treaty of Versailles. His speeches claiming that Germany now only wanted to pursue a peaceful foreign policy were rewarded when, the following year, Germany was allowed to enter the League of Nations and was given one of the permanent seats on the Council of the League. This showed that Germany was now seen as an equal, no longer an outcast, and recognised its status as a great power.

Historians have speculated whether the Republic was secure by the end of the 1920s. It could be argued that the government was meeting the needs of many of its citizens and winning grudging co-operation from its many

political parties. These were the lean years for the Nazi Party. As Cameron noted, 'Stresemann and his times denied the Nazi fire the oxygen of misery and it was all but extinguished.'

But despite these successes, the Weimar Republic still had serious problems. The fledgling government had not yet developed a system of parliamentary democracy that would survive and bring stability. There was division on social, economic, political and religious grounds amongst the strongest supporters of the republic, the Social Democrats, the German Democratic Party and the Catholic Centre Party. The army was only lukewarm towards the government and such indifference was also widely found in the civil service. As John Hiden noted in 1974 in *The Weimar Republic*, the army 'would tolerate the Republic for the time being in its own interests.' Finally, despite the apparent economic stability, the whole structure of the German economy was unhealthy. An over-reliance on foreign investments left the Weimar economy subject to the fluctuations of the international economy.

It will never be known whether the Weimar Republic could have gone on to win the loyalty of the German people or reversed the terms of the Treaty of Versailles, and so removed the shame of 1919, because it was not given the time. In 1929, the Wall Street Crash had disastrous consequences for the German economy and the Weimar Republic. As McKichan states, 'In 1929 it faced a disastrous economic blizzard in which much of what it had achieved was blown away.'

The Rise of the Nazis

Introduction

To understand how the Nazi Party was able to achieve success in Germany, it is necessary to look at the origins of the party, what it stood for, and how Hitler transformed it into an effective political force within Germany.

The origins of the Nazi party

The beginnings of the Nazi Party are to be found in the disillusionment that followed Germany's defeat at the end of World War One. Many small political groups emerged at this time and Hitler, now acting as a political instructor for the German army, was sent to investigate an obscure group by the name of the German Workers Party. This had been established by Anton Drexler and, despite its name, which indicated that it might be left-wing, it was not a socialist or communist group but instead was violently nationalistic (*völkisch* in German) in its outlook. Such ideas appealed to Hitler and he was invited to join the party. This seemed to give him the role in life he had been seeking since the end of the war. Such were his speaking skills that he soon came to dominate meetings. It has been argued that his success as a speaker was largely due to the intense sincerity of his nationalist beliefs and his ability to put into words the outrage and frustrations of millions of Germans over a variety of issues. He was able to influence the creation of new and more popular policies for the party and persuaded the members to change the name to the National Socialist German Workers Party (*Nationalsozialistische Deutsche Arbeiter Partei*), or NSDAP for short, in 1920. The following year Hitler became leader of the Party and helped to establish its own private army, the SA (*Sturmabteilung* or 'Storm-Troopers'). Their job at first was to protect party meetings from being interrupted by opposition groups, but later the SA was used for street demonstrations and parades.

The Nazi Party was only one of many so-called '*völkisch*' parties in Germany at this time. They shared common features such as being right-wing, nationalist in outlook, against the Weimar Government and bitterly opposed to the Treaty of Versailles. They also shared a common racist outlook in that keeping the German race pure was essential to maintain

Source 10.1

Hitler as a speaker at a mass rally.

the strength of the nation (*Volk*). The Nazis differed from the others because Hitler was convinced that his policies would save Germany and because of his abilities as a public speaker.

His ideas appealed to many in Bavaria in the immediate post-war era and membership of the party grew during 1922 to an estimated 20,000. With the onset of the period of hyper-inflation following the Franco–Belgian occupation of the Ruhr in 1923, with massive unemployment and the loss of savings during the period, many more were persuaded that the Nazis were the solution to their problems. Membership peaked at 55,000 just before the Beer Hall *Putsch* of November 1923. The writer Sir Ian Kershaw is firmly of the belief that, 'Hitler inspired the millions attracted to him by the conviction that he and he alone, backed by his Party, could lead Germany to new greatness.'

Hitler and his associates had made no secret of their desire to seize power within Germany. At a meeting in a Munich beer hall, the head of the Bavarian government, General Gustav von Kahr was sounding out his audience about the benefits of a dictatorship when Hitler crashed into the meeting, firing shots in the air and proclaiming that the Bavarian government had been overthrown and that he was now in charge.

The next day, led by Hitler and Ludendorff, the Nazis marched through the city towards the Bavarian War Ministry, believing that the military and the police would refuse to fire on the veteran general and would join the demonstration. As they entered a narrow street, shots were fired, the march broke up in confusion and Hitler was arrested and was charged with treason.

Hitler's arrest for the attempted *Putsch* should have been the end of his career, as he was charged with treason, a crime punishable by a life sentence. However, this was to be the start of his remarkable political career. He used his trial as a show-case for all that the Nazis represented and vented his anger on the authorities that appeared to be supporting the corrupt Weimar government. At his trial, he claimed to be a patriot rather than a traitor.

> *I alone bear the responsibility, but I am not a criminal because of that. If today I stand here as a revolutionary, it is a revolutionary against the revolution. There is no such thing as High Treason against the traitors of 1918.*
>
> — *Adolf Hitler, 1923.*

Source 10.2

Hitler during his imprisonment at fortress Landsberg, February to November 1924

A sympathetic judge and jury found him guilty but sentenced him to the minimum sentence of just five years. This contrasted starkly with the brutal slaying of Spartacists in 1919. In effect, Hitler served just under one year in rather comfortable surroundings in Landsberg Castle.

Another important consequence of the failed Beer Hall *Putsch* was that Hitler now realised that it was not possible to seize power illegally. The Germans had too much respect for law and order. He would have to achieve power by using constitutional means to undermine and overthrow the constitution. In addition, his allies had deserted him when the going had become tough. There would be no more pacts or compromises. Power would have to be achieved by the Nazis and the Nazis alone.

Working within the system

Hitler's release in 1925 found him looking at a changed Germany. Prosperity was beginning to return as a result of the Dawes Plan and, on the diplomatic front, Stresemann was making the case for Germany. Support for the extremist parties was in decline, and even within the Nazi Party the situation was hardly encouraging. Hitler set himself the aims of improving the efficiency of the party, developing the effectiveness of its organisation (particularly the propaganda machine) and reasserting his control over the party. Such was his success that Simpson has concluded that, 'By the end of 1926, Hitler's position [within the party] was unchallenged.'

His uncompromising stance against the Treaty of Versailles and the Weimar Republic as well as his oratorical skills placed him in a strong position when, after October 1929, the German people sought out a strong leader for Germany.

It was during his term of imprisonment in Landsberg Castle that Hitler dictated his book, *Mein Kampf*, to his secretary, Rudolf Hess. Till his suicide in 1945, Hitler never deviated from the ideas he had set out in this book which was part autobiography, part political beliefs. This formed the basis of the twenty five point action programme that would save Germany. Its main themes were:

- Nationalism – the Nazis called for all Germans to be united under one leader. Thus, Germans living in Austria, Czechoslovakia and Poland should be reunited in one Greater Germany. This point also emphasised that the Treaty of Versailles and the Treaty of St Germain (that had been signed with Austria at the end of World War One) should be destroyed.

- Anti-Semitism – the party was violently anti-Jewish in its outlook. Anti-Semitism had a long history within Germany and the identification of the Jews as an 'enemy of the state' was a theme familiar from the time of Bismarck. The Jews were blamed for strangling the German economy and being responsible for the 1923 hyper-inflation. They also were accused of 'stabbing the German army in the back' in 1918, and of being pro-communist in outlook. Such a group had no place in a pure Germany. Anti-Semitic ideology was used to justify the removal of citizenship from Jews, their exclusion from holding public office and their deportation from Germany.

- Socialism – At this time, the party supported the idea of measures against large industrialists and capitalists in order to help the small, independent trader and craftsman. Hitler paid lip-service to these ideas, probably in an attempt to win the support of these groups. Once in power, these ideas were quietly shelved and the Nazis never did anything which might threaten the prosperity of the German business community.

The Rise of the Nazis

- Social Darwinism – In this theory, the strongest survived while the weak did not. Hitler regarded the Germans as a master race, representing the highest degree of evolution. The converse of this was that there had to be an inferior race, since the Germans were superior to all others. Thus, Jews, negroes and the Slav races were relegated to serve their German masters and it would be necessary to control their numbers.

- Lebensraum – Germans would need space in which to expand their master race. This would be taken from the *Untermenschen* (sub-humans), particularly from the Slav lands to the east of Germany. This land would be taken by war, which was the supreme test of a nation's superiority. In *Mein Kampf*, Hitler argued that, 'Land and soil is the goal of our foreign policy.' Again he noted that, 'State boundaries are made by man and changed by man.'

Hitler called for the creation of a *Volksgemeinschaft* – a national community – in which the old divisions of class, religion and wealth would disappear with everyone working for the benefit of the people. Such a paradise could only be brought about by a strong leader. Democracy was regarded as weak, and in *Mein Kampf* Hitler outlined his case showing that only he could act as Germany's saviour. The years of waiting and preparation culminated in success following the onset of the depression in Germany. These talents and these beliefs transformed Hitler from the failed Viennese artist into one of the greatest figures of world history.

To whom did Hitler appeal during what was later called 'the period of struggle'? Shirer has argued that, 'Hitler, aided by a military caste, succeeded in inculcating a lust for power and domination, a passion of unbridled militarism, a contempt for democracy and individual freedom and a longing for authority, for authoritarianism.' Ritter takes the opposite point of view. He noted that, 'There is no doubt that the majority of educated Germans were very distrustful of the Hitler propaganda; very many felt that his political system was foreign to them.'

> "
> *The NSDAP was in the fortunate political position, unlike almost every other party in the Weimar Republic, of appealing to different groups for different reasons.*
>
> David Welch, The Third Reich – Politics and Propaganda, 2004.

The triumph of Hitler

Source 10.3

October 1929
Wall Street Crash.
US demands repayment of German loans.
German unemployment rises.

March 1930
Brüning of the Centre Party becomes chancellor.
Government tries to balance budget.
Cuts in pay of civil servants and unemployment benefits.
Brüning is forced to run Germany only by use of presidential decree – Article 48 of the Constitution.

September 1930
Reichstag elections. Nazis increase number of seats from 12 to 107. Communists also increase number of seats from 54 to 77. Fall in support for the SPD from 153 to 143 seats.

1930–32
Unemployment rises to 6 million.

April 1932
Presidential elections held. Hitler comes second to Hindenburg.

July 1932
Brüning is replaced as chancellor by von Papen. New elections held.
Nazi representation increases to 230. KPD numbers increase to 89. Fall in support for SPD to 133. No viable government can be formed.

November 1932
New *Reichstag* elections. Nazi seats fall to 196. KPD seats fall to 81. SPD seats fall to 121.

December 1932
von Papen is replaced as chancellor by General von Schleicher.
Political intrigue between von Papen and Hitler.

January 30 1933
Hitler appointed chancellor as head of a coalition government.

February 27 1933
Reichstag burns down in middle of election campaign.
Hindenburg signs decree for the 'Protection of the People and the State'.

March 5 1933
Nazis win 288 seats – only 43.9% of votes cast. Although banned, 12.3% of electorate vote for KPD. SPD won 120 seats. Therefore, the Nazis never won a majority in a free election.

"
Hitler would almost certainly have remained on the fringe of politics had it not been for the Great Depression, which began in 1929, and the hardship it brought.

Finlay McKichan, Germany, 1815–1939: The Rise of Nationalism, 1992.

The cause of the economic collapse which swamped Germany in the early 1930s is to be found on the other side of the Atlantic. Since the end of World War One, the USA had been enjoying a period of economic prosperity. This was shown by its eagerness to invest abroad, especially after the Dawes Plan of 1924. For Germany, this meant that its economic revival was dependent on US loans, many of which were of a short-term nature. With the collapse of the New York stock market in October 1929, the Americans demanded the return of their money. This set off a chain reaction in Germany which soon witnessed the return of mass unemployment and fears of a return to the hyper-inflation of 1923. This posed a difficult problem for the socialist-led coalition of the day.

Financial orthodoxy dictated that a government should not spend more money than it received in taxes. If tax revenue fell, in this case due to large numbers of people becoming unemployed, and government spending increased, due to an increase in payments of unemployment benefit, then the government would have to act to ensure a balanced budget. To this end, the socialists had to decide on whether to balance the budget by cutting unemployment benefit to many of its supporters, or to resign. Unable to take the difficult decision to cut payments, the last democratically-elected government of Germany till 1991 left office.

Source 10.4

Benefits queue in Hanover, 1930.

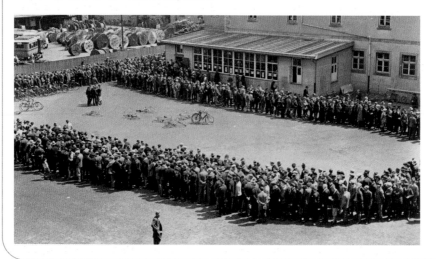

10

President Hindenburg had now to rely upon the use of Article 48 in order to ensure government business was undertaken. This set a dangerous precedent that the Nazis would later exploit to help establish their one-party state. A new government led by the Centre Party leader, Brüning, was now called upon to tackle the economic crisis. He decided to follow financial orthodoxy and cut both the benefits paid by the state and the salaries of government officials. This merely made the situation worse as government revenue fell further and there was an increase in government expenditure, thus leading the economy into a downward spiral. The following chart shows the increase in unemployment in Germany in a year on year basis.

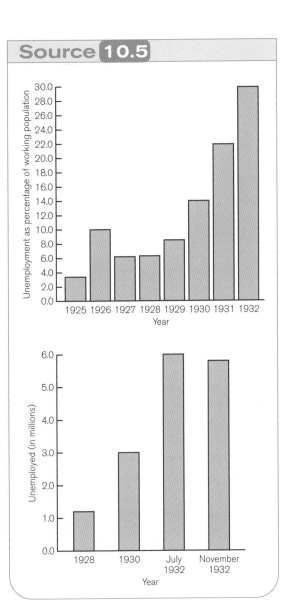

Source 10.5

There is no doubt that Germany suffered much more than either Britain or France during this period and that Hitler exploited this misery to the full.

Electoral support for the Nazis

> Its [the Nazis'] growing electoral support in the elections of 1930 and July 1932 was directly related to the growth of mass unemployment, and the growth of political instability, in this period.
>
> Mary Fulbrook, Hitler, 2004.

It is all too easy to see a direct correlation between the increasing rate of unemployment and the growth in support for both the Nazis and the communists. but recent research has shown that not all of the unemployed

Source 10.6 · *Mary Fulbrook, Hitler, 2004.*

Elections to the *Reichstag* (number of seats), 1928–1932

Party	May 1928	September 1930	July 1932	November 1932
NSDAP	12	107	230	196
DNVP	73	41	37	52
DVP	45	30	7	11
Zentrum	78	87	98	90
DDP	25	20	4	2
SPD	153	143	133	121
KPD	54	77	89	100

voted for the Nazis. Indeed, Catholics tended to remain loyal to their Centre Party, and the unemployed working-class supported the traditional parties of that class, the socialists and the communists.

Rather, it was fear of unemployment, rather than unemployment itself, which tended to make many people look to the Nazis as a way out of the crisis. Nazis polled particularly strongly amongst the farming and small-town lower middle classes, especially in the predominantly Protestant areas of northern and eastern Germany. McKichan in *Germany 1815–1939* argues that, 'It was in working-class districts of large cities that the Nazis did worst. Where the Nazis did best was in small towns and in the countryside, especially in the Protestant North'.

> The Party derived enormous benefit from its continued effort to win over the rural population during the crisis. To vote for Hitler was for many a rejection of the existing system and a belief that the NSDAP offered the only real hope of change for specific social groups in their own interest.
>
> John Hiden, The Weimar Republic, 1974.

In fact LE Jones has argued in *German Liberalism and the Dissolution of the Weimar Party System* (1988) that the NSDAP managed to win support from a wide cross-section of society in this time of crisis. At the peak of unemployment, even some of the working-class were prepared to give the Nazis a chance.

However, there is much more to the eventual Nazi success than just the economic situation, though this is considered to be the crucial factor.

Other reasons for the rise of the Nazis

Many theories have been put forward in order to explain why Hitler was able to achieve power by January 1933.

Firstly, there was the appeal of the Nazi Party. They offered something to everyone, even if their policies were contradictory. The workers were promised jobs and a fairer share of the national wealth (the socialist part of National Socialism). Businessmen were promised the destruction of Communism, a curb on the power of trade unions and more control over how they ran their businesses. Farmers were promised a fair price for their goods and also the removal of the threat of bankruptcy by reducing the power of the Jewish banks. At the same time, consumers were lured by the prospect of cheap prices for food. The army was promised the destruction of the Treaty of Versailles and a programme of rearmament.

The middle-class was offered the destruction of the Jewish banks which they blamed for having robbed them of their prosperity and savings. Many in the middle-class were also attracted by the Nazi promise to create a society based on merit, not birth or wealth.

The young, unemployed of Germany were offered hope in place of despair. Thus, as indicated above, these forces came together in the summer/autumn of 1932 and helped propel the Nazis into power.

Another factor worthy of note is the effective use of propaganda by the Nazis. David Welch in *The Third Reich – Politics and Propaganda* (2004) argues that people who voted for the Nazis did so not so much because of their conversion by propaganda, but because doing so would lead to a material improvement in their own situation. But McKichan believes that the role of Goebbels, in charge of Nazi Party propaganda, was vital in helping to spread the Nazi message. This was accomplished by a variety of methods. Goebbels knew that a crowd was basically conservative and usually fearful of change. Thus, a crowd which was fearful and disorientated was ripe for manipulation by his master, Adolf Hitler.

The Nazis exploited the new media of radio and cinema to get their message across, as well as the more traditional methods of political posters, marches and rallies and the newspapers. To this end, Hitler's alliance with Hugenberg, the newspaper and cinema chain owner, and the Harzburg Front offered him widespread publicity. Indeed, the authors of *The Growth of Nationalism* argue that, 'The Nazis were among the first to realise the persuasive power of this medium [cinema].'

Hugenberg's press and cinematic empire allowed the Nazis to reach a mass audience as this was the era when people went to cinema about twice a week.

Another aspect of Nazi success was their efficiency in election campaigns. The four general election campaigns, in addition to the two rounds of presidential voting in 1932, and the referendum on the Young Plan held in 1929, had given the Nazis plenty of time to perfect their election techniques. Rothnie has suggested that 'Never has any Party prepared for power more thoroughly than the Nazis during the period 1925–1933.' To this end, they used their greatest electoral asset, the public speaking abilities of Hitler himself. This has led the authors of *The Growth of Nationalism* to conclude that, 'He was the Nazi Party's greatest electoral asset.'

The SA were also used to great effect in the Nazis rise to power. The sense of lawlessness which the Nazis promised to end was, ironically, of their own creation. Street battles between the SA and the communist *Rotfrontenband* played on German respect for law and order. The SA also acted as a protection squad for Nazi rallies and meetings, preventing the sort of disruption they visited upon their opponents.

Sadly, the Weimar Republic and its politicians cannot escape responsibility for the success of Hitler and historians have long debated to what extent the political weaknesses of the Weimar Republic contributed to Nazi success. John Hiden argues that, 'Brüning took up the Chancellorship during a period of profound public disillusionment with the parliamentary system.'

> *A pattern was established of right-wing politicians believing that they could use the Nazis to bring about the sort of authoritarian Germany they wanted, but actually playing into Hitler's hands.*
>
> Finlay McKichan, Germany, 1815–1939:
> The Rise of Nationalism, 1992.

Some of the weaknesses were long-standing, as old as the Republic itself.

The inability of the SPD and the KPD to co-operate in the face of the threat posed by their opponents can be traced back to the bloody suppression of the Spartacist uprising of 1919. Rather than unite to face a common enemy, they continued to squabble over the nature of socialism that was appropriate for Germany. Indeed, the resignation of the SPD-led coalition in March 1930 over the proposed cuts in unemployment benefit led to the rule of Brüning and its associated difficulties. To ensure the continuance of government business, Brüning had no option but to rely upon the goodwill of President Hindenburg to use Article 48 to ensure legislation was enacted. This provided the Nazis with the means to destroy the Weimar Republic.

Added to this was the political intrigue among President Hindenburg, von Papen and General von Schleicher who were more interested in the setting up of an authoritarian government that would restore law and order than in maintaining democracy.

Bruening fell from power when he lost the confidence of the president, but when Franz von Papen succeeded Brüning he was unable to put together any real support in the *Reichstag*. The misjudgement of holding an election in the middle of such a period of crisis was shown by the staggering rise in support for the Nazis. The Nazis gained the largest single block of votes in the *Reichstag* but even so Hitler rejected the offer of the Vice-chancellorship despite belief in some Nazi quarters that Hitler had missed a golden opportunity to gain power. Behind the scenes, the fate of von Papen was sealed by the actions of General von Schleicher who, as well as playing politics, also warned that the army could not guarantee the safety of any German government. He replaced von Papen in December 1932. Unhappy at his dismissal, von Papen entered into an alliance with Hitler to oust von Schleicher. Fatefully, von Papen agreed to Hitler's demands to be made chancellor, with von Papen as his vice-chancellor. Never was a man proved so wrong than von Papen when he argued on the eve of Hitler's appointment as chancellor on 30 January 1933, 'We've hired Herr Hitler.'

Significantly for the future of democracy in Germany Hildebrand makes the point that, 'the Party was never returned to power by a majority of the German people.'

Source 10.7

Berlin Police arresting communists at the Berlin radio trade fair 1932.

From Chancellor to *Fuehrer*

The following timeline gives a brief outline of how Hitler was able to establish a single-party, one man rule in Germany by August 1934. However, more detail is needed.

Although Hitler was the head of a coalition government, with only two other Nazis as members of the Cabinet, he had no intention of sharing power with anyone. Well aware of German respect for law and order, achieving his objective would have to be seen to be legal. But any attempt to change the constitution required a two-thirds majority in the *Reichstag* and thus another election was called for early March 1933.

To ensure his success, Hitler had already appointed Herman Göring who controlled the police force across two-thirds of Germany and wielded immense power. To bolster state police forces, the SA and the SS (*Schutzstaffel* or 'protective squadron', a separate Nazi paramilitary force) were to be given the status of auxiliary police forces. The Nazi state now used all means at its disposal to attack its enemies.

Source 10.8

23 March 1933
With support from the DNVP, the Enabling Act (Law for Removing the Distress of the People and the Reich) is passed.
81 KPD deputies had been arrested; 26 SPD members were 'missing', meaning the Nazis can achieve the two-thirds majority needed.
The Government can now issue laws without the president's signature.

2 May 1933
All Trade Unions banned. Nazi Labour Front set up.

July 1933
Nazis reach agreement with the Roman Catholic church – priests not to take part in politics.
All political parties except Nazis banned.

January 1934
State governments abolished. Gauleiters (leaders of local branches of the Nazi Party) are appointed by Hitler.

30 June 1934
'Night of the Long Knives' – all opposition to Hitler within the Party is eliminated.

August 1934
Hindenburg dies. Hitler becomes president as well as chancellor and takes the title '*Der Fuehrer*' – 'Leader'

Hitler had always claimed that there had been a communist threat to seize power in Germany. This appeared to be the case when the *Reichstag* went on fire on the evening of 27 February 1933. This fire provided such a convenient excuse for the Nazis that it has long been suspected that they started it. It now appears that the fire was, in fact, set by a young Dutch communist tramp by the name of Marius van der Lubbe. Whatever the case, the Nazis used this happy coincidence to serve their own ends. Hitler declared that the fire was the signal for a communist uprising. Certainly President Hindenburg believed it to be the case, signing the most important of all of the emergency decrees – the Decree for the Protection of the People and the State. This was to remain in force till the collapse of the Nazi state in April 1945. Under it, enemies of the state could be arrested; the right of free speech and assembly could be withdrawn and the media censored. Finally, the state could, in an emergency, take over the powers of the separate German states or *Länder*. In the frenzy caused by the aftermath of the *Reichstag* fire, the election was held, the Nazis gaining 288 seats, representing only 43.9% of the popular vote.

Source 10.9

Reichstag Fire of 27 February 1933.

Hitler did not yet have the necessary two-thirds majority in the *Reichstag* to change the constitution. He used the Decree for the Protection of the People and the State to ban the Communist Party and the order was issued to arrest the 81 KPD members of the *Reichstag*. Hitler was closer to achieving his two-thirds majority to change the constitution. It was now proposed that Hitler be given emergency powers to rule single-handedly for four years. His remark that 'You gave the other parties 13 years, now give me 4' struck a chord with the German people. The Law for Removing the Distress of the People and the Reich (the Enabling Act) was passed in late March 1933. Despite the courageous opposition of the SPD who voted against the law, with 26 members of their party 'missing', it was not possible to stop its enactment. The Enabling Act allowed for emergency decrees to be issued without presidential authorisation. In effect, Weimar democracy was over.

> *The Nazis used the powers given by the Enabling Act to dispose of any organisation which might oppose or obstruct them and to ensure that people in positions of authority supported them.*
>
> *Finlay McKichan, Germany, 1815–1939: The Rise of Nationalism, 1992.*

Hitler now had to secure the exclusive authority of the Nazi Party within Germany and to remove all forces opposed to him.

His first actions were against opposition political parties and organisations. Trade unions were banned on 2 May 1933. In their place, a Reich Labour Front was set up under Robert Ley. All strikes were declared illegal and the Labour Front was given powers to fix wages. Opponents from within the movement were quickly arrested and sent to the newly established concentration camp at Dachau, close to Munich. Others saw the danger and kept quiet. This was followed by the banning of the SPD on 22 June. Most of the other political parties broke up, the last being the Catholic Centre Party which disbanded on 5 July 1933. On 14 July, a new law was passed declaring the Nazi Party the only political party allowed in the Reich. Hitler now tried to convince the German people that their destiny and that of his party were one and the same thing.

The professions were quickly brought under the control of the Nazis, with people seeking promotion learning that it was necessary to at least appear to support the policies of the Nazis. Many did believe in Nazi policies and in Hitler's ability to lead Germany to a brighter future. By 1936, 32% of teachers and an even higher number of doctors, 45%, were members of the Nazi Party.

Organised religion could have acted as a focus for opposition groups to the Nazis. On coming to power, the Nazi leadership feared that a conflict involving the churches might upset large numbers of Germans. Thus, initially, they followed a conciliatory policy towards religious worship and in July 1933 the Nazis reached an agreement with the Catholic Church. Under Hitler's *Concordat* the Catholic Church was guaranteed religious freedom and the right to run its own affairs without state interference. In return for these guarantees, the church pledged not to interfere in politics. This agreement suited both sides. The church felt it had protected its position, while the agreement helped to remove any lingering support for the Catholic Centre Party.

The Protestant faith was represented by 28 different churches that had a combined membership of 45 million. Hitler was to exploit these divisions to enforce his control on the Protestant churches. On 4 April 1933, Ludwig Müller was appointed as National Bishop to lead all the

Protestants in a German Christian Church. This new church was as equally dominated by Nazi beliefs as by religious teachings. Despite all attempts, the voices of opponents would not be stilled. Ministers such as Martin Niemöller and Dietrich Bonhoeffer showed great courage in speaking out against the Nazi regime. Nonetheless, by 1937 the Protestant churches had lost their ability to defend themselves against the state.

The major issue now facing Hitler was the position of the army and the role of the president. It was clear that President Hindenburg would not long survive. In order to declare himself *Fuehrer*, Hitler would require the support of the army. However, Ernst Röhm, the leader of the SA, was demanding that there be a 'second revolution' in which the army would be merged with the SA with the role of the army being limited to frontier duty and its other functions given to the SA. This posed a major threat to Hitler. The SA now numbered over two and a half million men who were used to street-fighting and the use of violence to achieve their aims. Having helped Hitler to achieve power, the SA now represented a threat to many within Germany whom Hitler could not afford to offend – particularly the army officers. Hitler needed to calm their fears and so began to consider the elimination of Röhm and the SA as a solution to his difficulty.

On 30 June 1934, the leaders of the SA were murdered, arrested or disposed of, as were other opponents to Hitler from within the Nazi Party. These included General von Schleicher, who had been chancellor briefly, prior to Hitler coming to power. On the other hand, Heinrich Himmler benefited from the Night of the Long Knives. His SS had helped with the arrests and subsequent murders of Hitler's opponents and after the 'Night of the Long Knives' there was a major shift within Germany towards a police state under Himmler's direction.

The full meaning of the Nazi chant, '*Ein Volk, ein Reich, ein Fuehrer*' now became totally clear to all. Hitler was the German state and any opposition would be ruthlessly destroyed.

Following the death of Hindenburg on August 2, 1934, the army kept their part of the agreement. Hitler proclaimed himself president as well as chancellor and took the title of *Fuehrer* or Leader. The Minister of Defence, Field Marshall Werner von Blomberg, insisted that all officers of the army pledge a personal oath of loyalty to the *Fuehrer* and this was critical in securing Hitler's hold on power. On 19 August 1934, in a plebiscite, 43.06 million Germans voted in favour of Hitler becoming *Fuehrer*. With the backing of 89.93% of the electorate, Hitler was now in a more secure position.

The significance of these times has been commented upon by several historians. Berghan has stated that the events from January 1933 had

completely transformed the political landscape of Germany and Simpson concluded that:

> *In a rapid series of moves, Hitler consolidated his own position, extended the authority of the Reich government over the individual German states and crushed all potential sources of opposition.*

The Nazis were now in control. What kind of Germany would they fashion?

Activity

Draw a spider diagram around the central question 'How did Hitler achieve power in Germany by 1933'.

Around your central question draw five boxes. Each box should contain ONE main reason why Hitler came to power. For example one of your boxes should contain 'weakness of the Weimar constitution'. From each of the boxes draw at least three more legs each one leading to a particular point which further develops the point made.

Develop each of the other four boxes you have in your diagram. When you have finished you have the information needed to explain why Hitler rose to power.

Exam essays

1 Why did Hitler become Chancellor in 1933?

2 How significant was resentment in Germany over the treaty of Versailles in Hitler's rise to power?

Germany under Hitler

Introduction

Hitler's aim was now to establish a country that reflected Nazi beliefs and ideology. This process was to be known as *Gleichschaltung* or co-ordination. So thorough was this process that Simpson has declared that, 'By 1939 the Nazi regime had extended its control over almost every social, professional and economic organisation and institution.'

Nazi control of civil life

Political parties had been outlawed and an agreement reached with the Catholic Church. The Nazi control of religion was further extended by the appointment of a *Reichsbishop* as head of the Protestant churches in Germany, although opposition to the regime was never completely eliminated.

For the civil service, Hitler chose to dismiss any anti-Nazi members and all Jewish officials were forced to resign their posts. This allowed many previously unemployed to gain work, thereby reducing German unemployment and allowing the Nazis to claim they had solved Germany's economic crisis. However, the Nazis did require an efficient civil service to enable government business to be conducted. On 7 April, the Law for the Re-establishment of the Professional Civil Service was announced. This law allowed for the dismissal of Nazi opponents but since the Nazis had come to power legally, there was no justification for obstructing their policies and the civil servants went about their daily business.

Within the legal system anti-Nazi judges were dismissed and replaced by those sympathetic to the regime. In a democracy, it is guaranteed that once appointed, judges are to be free of political interference. Such was not the case in Nazi Germany. In 1934, any cases involving treason (usually an attempt to overthrow or undermine the authority of the legal government) were to be heard by a People's Court led by reliable Nazi judges. In effect, enemies of the Nazis could now be disposed of with no respect for the rule of law. This was followed in 1935 by the passing of the law against 'Acts Hostile to the National Community'. This all-embracing law effectively allowed the Nazis to persecute their opponents in an apparently legal way. Finally, judges regarded as too lenient or who had not conducted trials properly were subject to reprimand. In this way, the rule of law in Germany was slowly undermined and the rights of German citizens were severely restricted. However, as David Welch wrote, 'Without being necessarily staunch Nazis, many judges and lawyers welcomed the Nazi regime in 1933 for their promise to restore a more authoritarian notion of "law and order".'

Before he came to power Hitler promised to create the *Volksgemeinschaft*, a 'national community', of interests which he had promised prior to 1933. Now, having gained power, did he achieve his aims?

Nazi youth policy

For Hitler the youth of Germany was the key to his setting up of a 'thousand year Reich'.

The aim of Nazi youth policy was to turn boys into soldiers and girls into submissive housewives and mothers. From 1933, parents were encouraged to enrol their children in huge state-run organisations. This became compulsory after 1939.

For boys at the age of 10, membership of the German Young People (*Deutsches Jungvolk*) was available. On reaching 14, they would graduate to the Hitler Youth (*Hitler Jugend*). Under the direction of Baldur von Schirach, all boys' groups were to come under the control of the Hitler Youth. Evidence of the success of these efforts can be seen in the fact that by 1936, some 60% of all young Germans belonged to some Nazi organisation. Activities including camping and shooting were designed to prepare the male youth of Germany for the next conflict.

Pressure on parents to enrol their children increased with the Hitler Youth being recognised as a department of the state. However, it was only in March 1939 that membership became compulsory.

The outlook of the Nazi regime to girls can only be regarded, at best, as very conservative and, at worst,

Source 11.1

Hitler Youth in front of symbols of the Nuremberg Rally

Reichsparteitag nürnberg

sexist. Similar to boys, girls joined the League of Young Girls (*Jungmädelbund*) at age 10 and moved on to the League of German Maidens (*Bund Deutscher Mädel*) at the age of 14. By 1936, this League of German Maidens had a membership of over 2 million girls. In both of these organisations, emphasis was placed upon the three Ks – *Kinder, Kirche, Küche* (Children, Church, Kitchen), which taught girls to accept their role as a mother and a wife in the new regime. At 17, girls could join the Faith and Beauty organisation, specialising in home economics and preparations for marriage.

It was crucial for the Nazi Party to win the support of young people if its aims were to be fulfilled and how effective the state was in indoctrinating the youth of Germany is an issue which has caused considerable historical debate. The traditional view is that most young people were willing participants in the Nazi youth organisations and were enthusiastic in their support of the state. However, this view has been challenged as other evidence suggests that the regime was only partly successful in its integration of young people. Many young people showed opposition by refusal to join the Nazi youth organisations. Instead they joined groups like the 'Swing Youth' or the Edelweiss Pirates who were often locked in battle with members of the Hitler Youth. However most of these groups can be categorised as teenage rebellion to authority rather than opposition to specific Nazi ideology.

Overall there can be little doubt that some young people were totally won over by the state and the excitement of the various activities that the youth organisations offered. However, by 1939 support was beginning to wane as the members became tired of the strict regimentation of the organisations and they became disaffected by the ineffective leadership.

Nonetheless, at the end of the war, with Germany on the verge of defeat, many young Germans sprang to the defence of the Fatherland – but did that mean they were Nazis or patriotic, nationalist Germans? The debate goes on.

Youth organisations and activities were some of the more subtle methods used to capture the minds of the German young and to indoctrinate them in Nazi methods and ideology. The other, more direct method, was by Nazi control of education.

Nazi education policy

Education was viewed as vital to secure the acceptance and continuation of the Reich. A first task was the purging of the teaching profession of any potential opposition to Nazi ideas. Jewish teachers were immediately dismissed from their posts. Teachers were encouraged to join the National

Socialist Teachers' Alliance (NSLB) whose task was, in effect, to indoctrinate teachers in Nazi beliefs. By the outbreak of war in 1939, the majority of teachers had attended at least one course run by the NSLB and many were enthusiastic members of the Nazi Party and wanted to share its beliefs with their young classes. Specialist schools were also set up. These included the so-called '*Napolas*', Nazi military academies where the emphasis was on military training. On leaving, pupils were expected to join the *Waffen SS*. The aim of the '*Ordensburgen*' schools was to train the next generation of Nazi leaders. Here there was a strong emphasis on political teaching. Higher education was also purged to ensure that Nazi ideology was not exposed to criticism or discussion.

Source 11.2

Raising the flag in school, 1941.

Sieg Heil!

The Nazis also altered the school curriculum to reflect their point of view. Sport, for example, was encouraged to produce a generation of fit recruits for the various military branches of the Nazi state. There was a strong emphasis on the teaching of history to show German students the glory of the German past and to encourage them to accept Nazi political ideas. Not surprisingly, given Nazi beliefs in racial superiority, biology teaching was changed to reflect Nazi ideology. In particular, there was great emphasis put on the teaching of racial stereotypes to show the supposed superiority of the Aryan race. *Rassenkunde* (racial studies) was a new subject introduced into the Nazi school curriculum. Even maths was subverted to serve the ideas of Nazi ideology. During this period, academic standards fell, as did the status which teachers had previously held. Now they were regarded as a tool of the state, rather than an independent profession.

Nazi economic policy

The Nazis had come to power during the worst economic depression to date. They claimed to have the answers to the economic ills facing Germany. It was therefore vital that the issue of unemployment in particular, and Germany's economic outlook, in general, should be tackled immediately.

In this situation, timing was everything. Unemployment in Germany was beginning to fall towards the end of 1932, as was electoral support for the Nazis. This was, in part, due to a general upturn in the world economy. Nonetheless, the Nazis took the credit for this improvement which was totally outside their control. Nazi dismissal of enemies of the state and many Jewish workers created jobs for unemployed Germans. Those who had been dismissed were simply not included in the unemployment statistics. But, by themselves, these measures would not have been enough. It is necessary to look at Nazi economic policy to see if they did achieve an economic miracle, as Goebbels often claimed.

The Nazis began a massive programme of public works that employed tens of thousands of Germans. Work schemes (*Arbeitsdienst*) introduced under the Law to Reduce Unemployment included the construction of the motorway network and between 1933 and 1936 the Nazi government spent 5 billion Reichmarks on public works. As men were taken on under these schemes, the economy would benefit as, firstly, they were now employed and not claiming benefits from the state, so government expenditure would fall. At the same time, they now entered the labour market and began to pay tax, increasing government revenue. With money to spend, they created demand in other areas of the economy for goods and services, thereby encouraging increased employment in these areas. The cumulative effect of these schemes is shown overleaf.

The architect behind the revival of the German economy was Hjalmar Schacht.

> " As long as I remained in office, whether at the Reichsbank or the Ministry of Economics, Hitler never interfered with my work. He never attempted to give me any instructions, but let me carry out my own ideas in my own way and without criticism... However, when he realised that the moderation of my financial policy was a stumbling block in his reckless plans (in foreign policy), he began, with Göring's connivance, to go behind my back and counter my arrangements.
>
> — *Hjalmar Schacht .*

Schacht was able to avoid inflationary pressures building up in the economy by a strict control of wages. Any shortage of money for the various schemes was simply printed, but wages were not allowed to match price increases. Given the control of the labour force by the Reich Labour Front, there was little that workers could do to alter this fact.

The aim of the Labour Front was to put the interest of the community and state before the needs of the individual. Until the outbreak of the war, most German workers found that there had been a slight decline in their overall standard of living.

Source 11.3

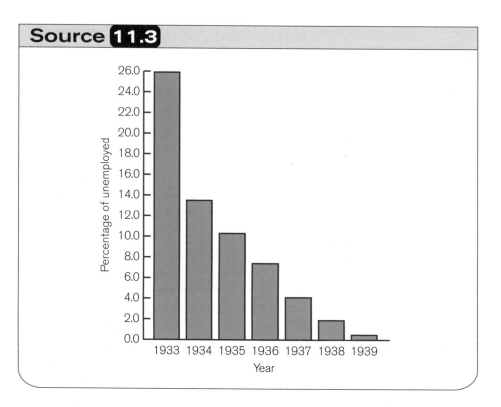

Source 11.4

Another factor contributing to German economic recovery was that, from the outset, the new regime began secretly re-arming Germany. For example, lorries ordered by the state were in fact military vehicles and the great firm of Krupp was engaged in an agricultural tractor programme that actually produced tanks. Contrary to the terms of the Treaty of Versailles, in 1934 virtually all of the planes produced were for the air force. In 1936, Göring

Construction of the Reich's Autobahn, 1933.

was put in charge of the re-armament programme. In a memorandum of August 1936, Hitler argued that Germany had two main aims.

> *1. The German armed forces must be operational within four years.*
>
> *2. The German economy must be fit for war within four years.*

Göring advocated the policy of 'guns before butter'. In other words, the German people would have to make some sacrifices in their standard of living to pay for re-armament that would ensure the safety of the Reich. Overall, the Nazi government had distorted the economy in order to prepare for war. In the short term, it certainly created jobs, but by 1939 there were severe pressures building up in the German economy.

In an attempt to deflect criticism from the regime caused by the decline in the standard of living, the Nazis set up organisations like *Kraft durch Freude* (KdF or Strength through Joy). Its aim was to provide loyal workers with rewards such as cruises or vacations at Nazi holiday camps. These were subsidised by the state and were later extended to cover theatre and use of sports facilities. The regime even tried to produce a people's car, or *Volkswagen*, which would be mass produced at reasonable prices. Although the first model appeared in 1938, increasing demands for military vehicles meant that this was never fully developed. Nonetheless, it has been estimated that by 1938, some 180,000 workers had been on a KdF subsidised cruise and that one third of the workforce had enjoyed a state subsidised holiday. Another attempt to persuade the workers that the Nazi state was delivering for them was the *Schönheit der Arbeit* (Joy at Work). This was an organisation that attempted to persuade employers to improve working conditions by, for example, providing better ventilation, improved lighting and providing workers with nutritional meals.

Despite all of these measures, there was still some unrest amongst workers, as was seen in strikes in Berlin in 1936 and increasing mistrust towards the government. The morale of these groups was always a worry to the regime and the government kept a watchful eye on working class districts. It proved impossible for the Nazis to end working-class loyalty to the socialist and communist parties.

> *The basic principle of National Socialist economic policy was to use the traditional capitalist structure with its competent economic bureaucracy to move towards its prime objective: acceleration of re-armament.*
>
> — *Karl Bracher.*

Hitler had gained power through the support of the middle-class, and, in particular, the lower middle-class. He promised to revolutionise German

society, sweeping away the class structure which was based on wealth and heritage and replacing it with a meritocracy, where promotion would be based on service to the Reich. This had been an important element in his propaganda prior to assuming the chancellorship. He identified with the host of shopkeepers, clerks and skilled craftsmen. This so-called *Mittelstand* welcomed Hitler's stabilising of the political and economic situation. Hitler appeased them by banning the opening of any new department stores from May 1933 and reducing competition in craft trades. State and party organisations were encouraged to provide preferential treatment to owners of small businesses. Despite this, the promise of a new class structure never really appeared. After all, Hitler depended on the traditional classes to help prop up his regime and provide leaders for the armed forces. The need to re-arm Germany also led to a dependence on big business and in the period until 1939, many small businesses were squeezed out as is shown by the decline in employment amongst self-employed craft workers of almost 500,000 between 1936 and 1939. Thus Nazi promises to this group remained unfulfilled.

Another important element in Nazi support prior to 30 January 1933 was the farmers of Germany. They had been badly affected by the collapse of world trade in 1929 and were facing crippling interest repayments to banks. Hitler had promised to get the 'bank Jews' off the backs of German farmers and to guarantee them fair and stable prices for their products. The farming class was viewed by the Nazis as the true representatives of the *völkisch* community and they advocated the policy of 'Blood and Soil' to symbolise this importance. Practical measures taken by the Nazis included increasing tariffs on food entering Germany from abroad and attempting to cancel the debts run up by farmers. Additionally, the government tried to prevent the disappearance of small farms and their absorption into larger units by the Reich Entailed Farm Law of September 1933. In effect this prohibited the sale of farms of around 30 acres as these were now declared to be hereditary and had to be passed on unchanged to the eldest son. Farmers were offered a range of financial inducements to stay on the land, and between 1934 and 1938 interest payments on farm debts had been reduced by £280 million. The reason for this state support of agriculture was obvious – the need for Germany to be self-sufficient to feed itself in time of war.

State direction was also evident in the operation of the Reich Food Estate. This became a massive organisation employing some 20,000 civil servants and was led by Walter Darre. Its function was to run the rural economy, fix prices and wages for the agrarian sector, establish food quotas and allocate available resources. By reducing food imports, the money saved could be diverted to help the re-armament of Germany. With all of these measures in place, income for farmers did recover in the short term but after 1937 farming came under increased pressure due to the need to feed a growing population that was slowly gearing up for war. Thus, despite all their efforts, the Nazis were unable to stop the drift away from the countryside as more and more left in search of a better living.

Nazi family policy

The Nazi view towards women was summed up in their slogan, *Kinder, Kirche, Küche* (Children, Church, Kitchen). The role of women in the Third Reich was to be a conservative one of looking after their husbands and having children. On assuming power, the Nazi Party wasted no time. The Women's Front (*Frauenfront*) was set up in May of 1933, under the direction of Robert Ley. All women's organisations were to expel any Jewish members, a task many of them were more than happy to carry out. Because of Nazi beliefs, women, especially in the professions, were under pressure from the regime. This included the virtual sacking of all women employed by either local or central government, and the dismissal of almost 15% of female teachers. Female lawyers also suffered a similar fate. This was extended in 1936 when it became law that no woman could serve as a judge and women were excluded from jury duty. Despite these efforts, however, female employment was to recover as Germany prepared for war by the end of the 1930s.

> "
> *The experiences of women varied dramatically… Here as in so many areas of the Third Reich, rhetoric and reality were often self-contradictory. Hitler's views on women, which now appear extraordinarily sexist, were at the time fairly representative.*
>
> — *Mary Fulbrook, Hitler, 2004.*

Hitler was obsessed by the need for German women to give birth to more children. In 1933, the regime embarked upon a policy designed to encourage an increase in the birth rate. Inducements such as a loan of up to 1000 Reichsmarks was offered to newly-wed couples, on the understanding that the wife would not seek employment. As the couple had children, the amount of loan to be repaid to the state was reduced by 25%. By 1937, the scheme had provided loans to nearly three-quarters of a million couples. There were tax reductions available for couples with children and family allowances were established for low-income families. Propaganda was also used to enhance the role of women. A Mother's Cross was established with mothers being awarded gold, silver and bronze crosses, depending on the number of children raised. Despite these efforts, the birth rate remained relatively stable, accounted for by shortage of housing and the fact that males were often absent for prolonged periods of time on service to the Reich.

> " *This rise [in births] was not necessarily a direct effect of Nazi policies; it can be explained in terms of increasing confidence in conditions of economic recovery; nor did the birth-rate fully recover to pre-Depression levels.*
>
> Mary Fulbrook, Hitler, 2004.

Hitler's racial beliefs also impacted on the role of women. Anxious to encourage the birth of the next generation of Aryan leaders, the regime encouraged women to have babies to members of the SS even if they were not married to them. The members of the League of German Maidens were indoctrinated to believe that this was their duty.

Despite Nazi emphasis on the traditional values of marriage, divorce rates actually rose between 1933 and 1939 from 29.7 divorces per 10,000 marriages to 38.3 per 10,000. Indeed, it became easier for men to divorce if they could show that their wife was immoral or refused to have children!

Part of the attempt to integrate women into the structure of the *Volksgemeinschaft* was the appointment in 1934 of Gertrud Scholtz-Klink as the National Women's Leader of the Third Reich. She helped to organise maternity schools for expectant mothers and encouraged the study of home economics. Thus, Nazi organisations like the National Socialist Womanhood and German Women's Enterprise were part of the state apparatus for the integration of women into the ideology of the Third Reich.

Internal opposition to the Nazis

Despite their claims to the contrary, the Nazis were never quite able to silence opposition to the regime. The churches provided some opposition to Nazi policies, despite severe persecution of their beliefs. However, opponents were never able to establish a single organisation to channel their resistance. Given the nature of the police state, with the *Gestapo* (short for *Geheime Staatspolizei*, secret state police) and the use of paid informers, this is not too surprising. Anyone opposing the regime was liable to severe penalties, not just for themselves but for their families as well. Thus, to voice opposition to the regime involved a considerable degree of personal courage.

Initially, opposition to the Nazis came from traditional quarters. The communists and socialists continued to resist, albeit via secretive means. This opposition was ineffective due, in large measure, to the speed of the Nazi takeover of power and to the ruthlessness of the regime towards its opponents. The Dachau concentration camp was opened less than a month after Hitler came to power. The opposition also lacked a national leader and had no armed supporters to call upon in their efforts to resist the government. Hitler was also able to use fear of a communist plot to scare the German people into submission. Their efforts were further hampered by communist refusal to co-operate with the socialists over issues which had existed since World War One. The situation was also compromised by Stalin's secret support of the Hitler government. Taking orders from Moscow, Germany's communists had followed Stalin's orders to attack other socialists rather than oppose the Nazi regime. The USSR was Germany's most important trading partner during the 1930s and Stalin did not want to see this changed. He

Source 11.5

Prisoners working as part of a construction team in Dachau concentration camp, 1938.

firmly believed that Nazism was a passing phenomenon that would collapse, leaving the way open for the establishment of a communist regime in Germany. Thus, German communist organisations were told to play a waiting game and to be ready for their opportunity.

Even within the army, some officers looked with contempt on 'Corporal Hitler' and despised his upbringing. To an extent the army's suspicion of Hitler was eased after the 'Night of the Long Knives' of 30 June 1934, but after discussions in the winter of 1937 about the aims and objectives of Nazi foreign policy, some generals voiced opposition to the plans on the grounds that Germany was not yet ready for war. Hitler took this criticism personally and the army was purged. Von Blomberg was forced to resign as Minister of Defence and head of the army in February 1938 and Hitler appointed himself as army supreme commander. The Chief of the Army High Command, General Fritsch was also forced to resign following accusations of a homosexual affair. His replacement was General von Keitel as Chief of the High Command and General von Brauchitsch as Commander-in-Chief of the army. Thus, Hitler's control of the army was now assured, at least until the tide of war turned against the Nazis in 1944. It was the army that came closest to the removal of Hitler in that year with the July bomb plot.

Nazism and Anti-Semitism

For most people, the Nazi dictatorship is linked forever to the persecution of the Jews and, uncomfortable as it may be, the anti-Semitism of the Nazi state was a factor in its popularity with many Germans. From its beginning, the Nazi Party was violently anti-Semitic. Once in power the Nazis sought first to isolate, then discriminate against and ultimately destroy the Jews living within Germany's borders.

> "
> Anti-Semitism was not only the core of Nazi ideology, but the Jewish stereotype that developed from it provided the focal point for the feeling of aggression inherent in the ideology.
>
> David Welch, The Third Reich – Politics and Propaganda, 2004.

In April 1933, the government organised a nationwide boycott of Jewish businesses. An article in the Nazi newspaper the *Völkischer Beobachter* made clear what was expected.

> "
> Boycott committees against the Jews throughout the whole Reich. On 1 April, at the stroke of ten, the boycott of all Jewish businesses, doctors, lawyers begins – ten thousand mass gatherings. The Jews have declared war on 65 millions, now they are to be hit where it hurts them most.
>
> Völkischer Beobachter, 30 March 1933.

A whole range of legislation was to follow.

On 7 April, 1933, Jews were dismissed from posts within the civil service. Four days later, they were banned from practising law. This was to be the beginning of a whole range of moves against the Jewish professions. Doctors, teachers and dentists, among others, were prohibited from working. In October 1933, a new law forbade Jews from working in journalism. Following this battery of legislation, there was a period of relative quiet in this area. Hitler may have wished to maintain some semblance of goodwill from abroad and to consolidate his position at home after August 1934.

1935 was to mark a crucial time in relations between the Jews and the state.

The keystone of Nazi policies towards Jews was announced in the Nuremberg Laws of September 1935. Under these, Jews were stripped of their German citizenship and marriage or sexual relations between Germans and Jews was also outlawed. Persecution of Jews now continued to escalate, despite a temporary respite during the 1936 Berlin Olympics when the Nazis tried to show only the positive side of the regime to the

Photo **11.6**

Park bench in Berlin with the inscription "Only for Aryans".

world. Such attacks were to lead to the frenzy of '*Kristallnacht*'. Using the excuse of the murder of a German diplomat in Paris by a Jew, the regime was determined to punish Jews within Germany. Shops and homes belonging to Jews were attacked, as were many synagogues. It has been estimated that up to 100 Jews were murdered during this 'night of broken glass'. In addition, a further 20,000 were sent to concentration camps. Despite Nazi propaganda arguing that the events of 8–9 November 1938 were the spontaneous response of the German people to events in Paris, it was quite clear that the attacks on Jewish property were organised by a small group led by Goebbels. In a secret Nazi report compiled prior to the events of *Kristallnacht*, it was shown that this was all planned.

> *The Fuehrer, at Goebbels' suggestion, had decided that such demonstrations were not to be prepared or organised by the party, but neither were they to be discouraged if they originated spontaneously…*
>
> *The oral instructions of the Reich Propaganda Director were probably understood by all the party leaders present to mean that the party should not outwardly appear as the originator of the demonstrations but that in reality it should organise them and carry them out.*
>
> — *Völkischer Beobachter, 30 March 1933.*

Kristallnacht led to conflict within the party hierarchy as Göring, in charge of the campaign of 'Guns before Butter' was shocked by the dislocation that might be caused to the economy. It was he who argued that a more systematic way had to be developed to deal with the Jewish question. The

regime also introduced new laws excluding Jews from participation in the economic life of Germany; Jewish pupils were expelled from schools and, in the light of these events, many now sought salvation in the form of emigration from a country that so obviously threatened their existence.

It is important to bear in mind that the policies of the regime between 1933 and 1941 were not part of some long-term plan to deal with the 'Jewish question'. Also no evidence exists to support the idea that all Germans in 1933 were in favour of any extremist or violently anti-Semitic policy. In *A Social History of the Third Reich*, Richard Grunberger argued that *Kristallnacht* divided Germany into three distinct sections of opinion, 'The shocked but silent at one end, the looters and vicarious sadists at the other – and a broad middle stratum of inert bystanders.'

Source 11.7

A looted Jewish shop in Berlin.

The police state

In order to ensure the obedience of the people and acceptance of his will, Hitler and his associates set about creating the apparatus of a police state. Concentration camps were supposed to be 'temporary places of arrest' till opponents of the regime could be 're-educated'. In reality, they were to become a feared institution of the Reich. The regime was able to portray the inmates of these camps as 'enemies of the state' and won the grudging approval of a populace that accepted that most of the inmates were people of whom they disapproved anyway. Certainly, reports at the time indicated that the secret police was eagerly supported by large numbers of people willing to denounce their friends and neighbours. Whether they were or not, the secret police or *Gestapo* seemed to be everywhere watching and listening. But the real enforcers of the Nazi state were members of the SS.

The SS was the state's internal security service, its purpose being to root out any opposition, real or imagined, to the will of the *Fuehrer*. This had been set up in 1925 to act as Hitler's personal bodyguard. However, in the period from 1933 it grew into a powerful, disciplined force, fanatically loyal to Hitler and ably led by Heinrich Himmler. With its distinctive,

threatening black uniforms and lightning flash collar symbols, it struck fear into the minds of most Germans.

It was later to provide guards for the concentration camps and to provide special squads to fight alongside the regular army. Its role would be greatly expanded after the outbreak of World War Two when it was to occupy large areas of conquered territory and to run the death camps of occupied Europe. Gordon Craig has concluded that, 'The force that prevented the regime from dissolving into chaos was terror and its instrument was the SS.'

In conclusion, opposition to the Nazis came from a variety of sources, encompassing social, religious and political areas. The motives were as varied as the opposition groups. However, there were many weaknesses in their opposition. Perhaps most important of these was the failure to realise that only by removing Hitler could the Nazis be overthrown and that was extremely difficult for any underground opposition to achieve. They lacked a common aim, leadership and organisation. Fundamentally, too many Germans supported the regime, even if only partly, to ensure any success for its opponents. To compound this, Nazi success in foreign policy led to even more supporters for the regime.

Nazi foreign policy

Nazi foreign policy remained consistent until the destruction of the regime in 1945. It was based on opposition to the Treaty of Versailles which was looked upon as a national humiliation and which Hitler was pledged to destroy. Additionally, in *Mein Kampf*, Hitler demanded that the German people be given the space needed to ensure the survival of the Aryan race. This space, or *Lebensraum*, was to be created from the Slavic lands to the east of Germany and ultimately from Russia. This was outlined in *Mein Kampf* where Hitler wrote, 'We take up where we broke off six hundred years ago. We stop the endless German movement to the south and west, and turn our gaze to the land in the east.' Lebensraum also had a practical aim – the gaining of resources available in Russia. With the re-armament of the regime after 1935, Germany needed access to ever more raw materials like coal and oil. Thus, Hitler's foreign policy was also motivated by economic needs.

Hitler's foreign policy was hugely popular in Germany, especially when he seemed to be reversing the humiliations of Versailles and the Weimar years.

His decision to end all reparations payments (although it should be noted that this had already been agreed with his Weimar predecessors) was portrayed as a great foreign policy achievement. In October 1933, Hitler announced Germany's withdrawal from the League of Nations and, more significantly, from the disarmament conference being held in Geneva. In

January 1935, as agreed at Versailles, a plebiscite was held in the Saarland to decide if the area should be restored to Germany. The Nazis used every means at their disposal to ensure a 'yes' vote, and the result, with 90% supporting a return to the Reich, was seen at home as another endorsement of the regime. In the spring of the same year, Hitler announced that Germany would no longer be bound by the military terms of the Treaty of Versailles. The army was to be increased in size. Despite threats from France, Hitler was able to escape punishment by offering Britain a deal on the size of the navies of both countries. This was made clear in his instructions to the German negotiators of the 1935 Anglo-German naval agreement.

> ❝
>
> *An understanding must be reached between the two great Germanic peoples through the permanent elimination of naval rivalry. One will control the sea, the other will be the strongest power on land.*
>
> *Adolf Hitler, 1935.*

Thus, Hitler was able to play the Allies off against each other, leaving him free to act.

In March 1936, Hitler ordered the re-militarisation of the Rhineland. Now known to be a gamble, the failure of France and Britain to defend its obligations under the Versailles Treaty ensured not only public acclaim for Hitler at home, but also saw his dominance of the army increase.

Source 11.8

Lands lost at the Treaty of Versailles and lands regained by the Nazis prior to the war.

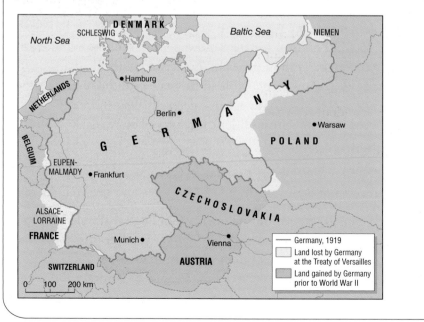

The foreign policy aims of the regime in the second half of the 1930s were made clear by the Hossbach Memorandum.

> "
> *The aim of German policy was to make secure and to preserve the racial community and to enlarge it. It was therefore a question of space… Germany's problem could only be solved by means of force and this was never without risk.*
>
> *Adolf Hitler, Hossbach Memorandum, November 1937.*

This led to an ever-more aggressive and expansionist foreign policy.

Despite its being forbidden by the Treaty of Versailles and the Treaty of St Germain, Hitler accomplished the *Anschluss* (union) with Austria in March 1938. His 'invasion' was endorsed in an April 1938 plebiscite, with 99.75% of Austrians voting in favour of Hitler's actions.

Finally, in September of 1938 Hitler was able to gain the Sudetenland of Czechoslovakia, with its majority of German-speaking citizens. At this point, Hitler had achieved almost complete control over the German people, and he began to believe his own propaganda that he was infallible. The rest of Czechoslovakia was swallowed up in March of 1939, again with only criticism but no action from Britain and France. With the Nazi–Soviet Pact of August 1939, Hitler had secured the neutrality of the USSR for his attack upon Poland.

Although Hitler's foreign policy successes were portrayed by Goebbels' propaganda machine as evidence of the infallibility of the *Fuehrer*, Hitler was an opportunist. He was skilful in being able to recognise opportunities in foreign affairs, like his abandoning of the military terms of the Treaty of Versailles in early 1935 to the fury of the French while negotiating with Britain on a naval agreement; exploiting weaknesses in his opponents; and capitalising on events as they arose.

Given this range of stunning foreign policy triumphs, especially in

Source 11.9

First Reichstag session following the 'Ausschluss', 1930.

comparison with the years of failure of Weimar, it is not surprising that the voices of opposition to Hitler were struggling to be heard. With better living standards and Germany now recognised, once more, as a great power, few in the country were willing to support calls for Hitler's removal from power. As noted by David Welch, 'Much of Hitler's popularity after he came to power rested on his achievements in foreign policy.'

Conclusion

Like many aspects of Nazi life, the experiences of various sections of the population varied, according to their degree of acceptance of, or opposition to, the regime. Nazi racial and foreign policies did bring about fundamental changes in German society but the so-called 'social revolution' demanded by Röhm and his supporters did not develop during the period of the Third Reich. His legacy was entirely negative; mass murder, the beginnings of a Cold War and the division of Germany until the last decade of the twentieth century.

Activity

Select ONE of the activities suggested at the end of the previous chapters and adapt it to deal with the Nazi State between 1933 and 1939.

Exam essays

1 The Nazi state between 1933 and 1939 maintained its power by the use of fear, force and rewards. Do you agree?

2 'A total dictatorship'. To what extent is this an accurate description of the power of the Nazi state in Germany 1933–1939?

Index